CHOOSING GLEE

CHOOSING GLEE

by Jenna Ushkowitz and Sheryl Berk

10 Rules
TO FINDING INSPIRATION,
HAPPINESS,
AND THE REAL YOU

St. Martin's Griffin

New York

www.stmartins.com

Designed by Georgia Rucker

Photo credits: All photos courtesty of author except: vi, 27, 60, 62-63, 65, 96, 104 (bottom left), 129, 132, 156-7, 159 (top), 165, 174-5, 188-189, 191, 193, 198-9, 209, 211 (top, midddle), 212-3, 214-5 courtesy of Fox Broadcasting Company. Photograph on page 126 courtesy of Adrian Finkel.

ISBN 978-1-250-03061-0 (trade paperback)
ISBN 978-1-250-03062-7 (e-book)

Griffin books may be purchased for educational, business, or promotional use. For information on bulk purchases, please contact Macmillan Corporate and Premium Sales Department at 1-800-221-7945 extension 5442 or write specialmarkets@macmillan.com.

First Edition: May 2013

10 9 8 7 6 5 4 3 2 1

This book is dedicated to Mom, Dad, and Gregg for teaching me how to march to the beat of my own drum.
—Jenna

contents

Theater camp, summer 2002

"Jazzercise time, but snack first!"

I'm ready for my close-up!

INTRODUCTION

i have always been a naturally happy person—maybe (to quote the great Gaga) I was born this way. My parents adopted me from Seoul, South Korea, when I was three months old. My mother says the first time she saw me in JFK Airport, I was napping peacefully after my twenty-four-hour journey to America. She took me in her arms, I opened my eyes, and I grinned from ear to ear.

I grew to be the comic relief in the Ushkowitz family, running around our Long Island home with pots and pans on my head singing at the top of my lungs. My parents hardly knew what hit them! They are not hams; they're not people who love the spotlight. But all I ever wanted to do was perform. Other

Me in Pre-K

parents might have been freaked out or frustrated by this, but not mine. Even though singing and dancing wasn't their thing, they were 110 percent behind me following my passion. Even if they didn't completely understand it, they were willing to trust me. My happiness was paramount. If I said I wanted to grow up and be a tightrope walker or a zookeeper, I think they might have actually let me give it a go. I am who I am because of who they are.

we are family

As individuals, my mom and dad are very different people who complement each other. When she was younger, my mom, Judi, was a secretary in NYC. After she got married and my brother, Gregg, was born, she gave up her job to care for her family. She never regretted it. She was so happy giving her children what she never had. Her parents were never very well-off, so she liked spoiling us with attention and gifts. Whatever we wanted, she got it for us: a life-sized Barbie doll, American Girl dolls up the wazoo, a Game Boy, and every video game in existence. She was so proud that she

Mom and dad

"Jenna always brought tears to my eyes no matter what she did because of her sheer determination."
—JUDI USHKOWITZ, MY MOM

2

could give us those things. She gave us all the love and attention a kid could ask for.

My dad, Brad, is a salesman for transportation. He basically sells eighteen-wheelers on the road to companies to ship their freight. He worked out of our home, so he was always there for us as well. When he took me to auditions, I remember he would work out of the car on the phone. He educated me in music, though he never had any formal training in it. He has such a wide range of songs that he knows and loves, everything from Motown and the Beatles to Billy Joel. Every time one of these songs pops up on *Glee*, I get such a kick out of it. My thoughts immediately take me back to rocking out with my dad to the car radio.

My brother Gregg is nine years older, but that's never come between us. I was always his "buddy," his wingman. He taught me dirty words to say on cue. (I owe my sailor mouth to him.) He showed me how to stick a Cheerio up my nose and blow it out. (Unfortunately, one time I sucked it in so hard it got stuck, and I had to go to the emergency room!) Gregg was always the troublemaker. I remember him blowing up my Barbies in the backyard.

"SHE HAD HER HEART SET ON A GOAL AND SHE WAS WILLING TO DO WHATEVER IT TOOK TO GET HER THERE."
—GREGG, MY BIG BRO

Brother Gregg and me

3

Nonetheless, he was thrilled to have a little sis who would laugh at his jokes. Gregg's a natural comedian and a whiz at impressions, but he went into insurance, a much more stable career than I chose! He's my cheerleader, and when I need it, my date. I took him to the GRAMMYs one year, and he lost his mind. He's a huge groupie.

My family never made an issue out of the fact that I was adopted. There was no "sit-down," no "breaking the news." It was just a part of who I was, a positive, not a negative. I know a lot of adopted kids want to search for their birth mothers. But I never had that urge—not even today. I felt completely whole and fulfilled in my family. My parents and brother made me feel loved, needed, wanted, and appreciated. I may have been born happy, but they made sure I stayed that way.

i oughtta be in pictures

My parents quickly discovered that I was an innate extrovert. Every time we went out to the diner, I'd go up to all the tables and say "Hi" to anyone who would acknowledge me. When I was just three, I started bugging my parents about being on TV. It looked fun and easy, so why I couldn't I do that? They took me to a commercial agent on Long Island. His name was Chicky, and he would always send me chocolate-covered matzo at Passover because he thought I was Jewish. I let him believe it because I loved the matzo so much, but the truth is my family is Catholic. My father's father was Jewish (hence the name "Ushkowitz"), but his mother was Catholic, and that's how he was raised.

Just hanging with Bill Cosby, for our watermelon Jell-O commercial.

My first job!

Thanks to Chicky, it didn't take me long to land my very first ad campaign. It was for Playskool's Dress Me Up Ernie doll. I thought it was the coolest thing ever. I still have the photo, and I want to blow it up and hang it in my apartment. Next, I did a Toys R Us commercial, and I got to wear a pink tutu (my own personal costume!) and wave. But my big break came when I was cast to jiggle with Bill Cosby on his Jell-O Jigglers commercials. I did them over a span of several years: the first when I was four, then again when I was six for watermelon Jell-O, and the last one, for Jell-O yogurt when I was eleven. I seemed to book gigs according to the rule of threes. I also did three Burger King commercials and three Hess Truck commercials. (Google these if you wanna laugh!)

I did over one hundred commercials, and truth be told, I got a little bored with it. I needed a challenge. So I moved on to auditioning for acting roles and (maybe thanks to my intimate relations with Dress Me Up Ernie?) I landed a role on *Sesame Street* when I was six. For three years, I was a recurring character. I worked with almost all the *Sesame Street* puppets: Big Bird, Snuffleupagus, Elmo, the Count, and Oscar. But my first day on set didn't go as smoothly as I would have liked. I was on antibiotics for strep, and my dad gave me waffles with sticky syrup for breakfast. I never liked syrup, so I refused to eat much, and I threw up all the way to *Sesame Street*. (Never, I repeat never, take antibiotics on an empty stomach!) My dad wanted to turn the car around, but I was determined, as sick as I was, to go. I reported to the set in Astoria, Queens, to work with Oscar and Slimey. The scene required me to plop down on a seesaw and propel Slimey into the air and across the playground into Oscar's trash can. Gordon wound up picking me up and dropping me down on the seesaw about twenty times to get the shot. By the time the director called "Wrap!" I was so nauseous, I couldn't see straight. I thought about hurling right there and then (Gordon was probably grateful I didn't!), but I managed to run off set and throw up in my Barney lunchbox.

My next big career move—minus the puppets—was on Broadway in the 1995 revival of *The King and I* starring Donna Murphy and Lou Diamond Phillips. I played "Princess Sunny Smile." At least that's what the cast and crew called me because I always came on stage to "The March of the Siamese Children" beaming. This was a serious job for an eight-year-old.

Me in The King and I

Daddy Lou and I

Opening night on Broadway! Mom, Dad, Lou, and me.

IK0404E MEZZ E 23 ADULT
EVENT CODE SECTION/BOX ROW SEAT
$ 70.00 MEZZ LEFT All Taxes Incl. if Applicable
PRICE @ ALL TAXES INCL. 70.00
MEZZ. RODGERS & HAMMERSTEIN'S
SECTION/BOX THE KING AND I
A 9X NO REFUNDS/NO EXCHANGES
ROW NEIL SIMON THEATRE
E 23 250 W. 52ND ST., NYC
SEAT THU APR 4, 1996 8:00PM
ST402A
3APR96

There was no time for school: I had eight shows a week, with two on Wednesday and two on Saturday. My dad bought a minivan so I could recline in one of the captain's seats and sleep on the way home. We didn't get home till midnight, and I had to be at school by 9:00 a.m. It was grueling, but it was one of the best experiences in my life. It taught me that showbiz isn't very glamorous at all: It's hard work. But it made me even more determined to follow this path. Hearing the applause, moving an audience to laugh or cry . . . I knew it was what I wanted.

Bill and I hanging, after our Jell-O yogurt commercial shoot.

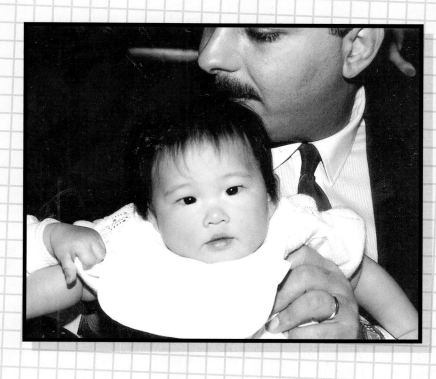

Dad and Gizmo,
my childhood pup

DAD SAYS

"Jenna's Korean name
Min Jee means strong willed—and she has always lived up to her name!
When she wants something, you better step aside because she will knock
you over. You just can't argue with her. When she was around two years
old, Jenna hated to go to sleep and always gave us a hard time. One night
she kept refusing, saying she wasn't tired and didn't need to get into bed.
As much as I pleaded with her to lie down, she refused. So I left her in our
room. When I came back several minutes later, I found Jenna fast asleep,
standing up with just her head on the edge of the bed. I guess she won."

Tina then...

come on get happy

I also "won" when I landed the role of Tina Cohen-Chang on *Glee*. Some people might dream of winning the lottery. My dream was to be on a hit TV show that makes people think and feel. And that's exactly what I got: *Glee* is more than just a dramedy filled with splashy musical numbers and the occasional Britney Spears tribute. It's had an incredible impact on everyone who is a part of it, and everyone who tunes in, week after week. It celebrates individuality, diversity, and the power of positivity. So yes, I feel lucky/blessed/on top of the world to be able to lend my voice to this incredible, ground-breaking show.

Tina now...

The irony of playing a bitter, angry Goth girl does not escape me. In the beginning, Tina dressed in black with fingerless gloves and fake-stuttered her way through McKinley. She was truly the anti-Jenna. For some reason, Ryan Murphy, Brad Falchuk, and Ian Brennan, *Glee*'s creators, cast me in the role, soon learning (surprise!) that I was a bubbly, positive twenty-two-year-old. For that reason, Tina's evolution included a serious attitude adjustment. She's in a lighter, more confident place. But I've always seen her as a positive person underneath all those dark, Goth clothes, and as the writing would lend, she just had to make the decision to stop bitching and hiding and be happy.

For some reason, Ryan Murphy, Brad Falchuk, and Ian Brennan, *Glee*'s creators, cast me in the role, soon learning (surprise!) that I was a bubbly, positive twenty-two-year-old.

WHAT GLEE MEANS TO ME
BY BRAD FALCHUK
(co-creator of *Glee* and cool dude)

In my experience, the only real path to joy and happiness is truth. Most of our problems in life do not stem from an issue (I didn't get into the college I wanted, I couldn't buy that shirt I loved, that guy dumped me) but from our inability to see the issue for what it is (my strengths lie in areas that school doesn't value, I have chosen to spend my money elsewhere, he was gay all along).

If we can find the truth in a situation, find our true feelings about it, we can transform our relationship to it and find growth and joy even in failure and especially in success.

The act of singing and dancing is about as true a form of self-expression as we have access to as human beings. It's not about the quality of your pitch or the precision of your rhythm. It's about finding an emotion inside of you and sending it out into the world untouched by reason and unbroken by self-awareness. Ask a bunch of first graders who can sing or who can dance and every hand goes up. Because everyone can sing and everyone can dance, just like everyone can tell the truth. We may choose not to—out of fear of being judged—but we all can.

That is the message I am trying to impart through *Glee*. Sing. Dance. Be true. Find joy in those pure moments of self-expression. Let them radiate to every other moment in your life and help you find truth and happiness no matter what you are doing. No matter what you are afraid of. It may be a cliché, but the truth will set you free!

Which brings me to the point of this book: Yes, you can *choose* glee. I did; Tina did; you can. It's not like ordering off a menu: "Gee, today I'll have the happiness special. . . ." Instead, it's a conscious decision every day to seek out positivity. It's been my lifelong quest: I'm like the Don Quixote of Practical Happiness or something! I truly believe that no one is a lost cause. Everyone has the power to be positive, no matter what his or her circumstances. You can complain about all the stuff you've been through . . . or you can look on the bright side. I pick the latter. I don't see the sense in dwelling on bad decisions or bad moods. Every day is a new day and a new chance to do something different: to get unstuck, to find your true calling, to surround yourself with people who lift you up instead of bring you down.

I always knew that I would eventually find the place where I belonged in this world. Right now that's on *Glee*, surrounded by these ridiculously talented actors. But I won't lie and tell you that I never cried, never doubted, never felt lost. I did—more times than I care to recall. I made mistakes. I took the wrong road. I forgot to BREATHE.

There were dark times along the journey to where I am now, but I wouldn't be the person I am without those experiences. I've come out stronger and wiser. I wouldn't know this joy without experiencing those moments of despair, confusion, and the feeling that no one in the world understands. I hope this book will help you do the same.

> I took the wrong road. I forgot to BREATHE.

A biting comedy for the underdog in all of

The first posters of us we sighted on the streets!

PREVIEW EVENT AFTER AMERICA
TUE MAY 19

PREVIEW EVENT AFTE
TUE MA

On a boat on the way to the O2 in London. We travel fancy.

Jessie and I at the Superbowl in Dallas.

15

MG0130M MEZZ
$ 25.00
EVENT CODE
PRICE & ALL TAXES INCL
SECTION/BOX
ROW J 102
SEAT

MEZZ
MEZZANINE
CA 17X
J 102
MIN4013
30JAN05

NO EXCHANGES/NO REFUNDS
All Taxes Incl. If Applicable
ADM 8
J-TYPE JRUSH
FIDDLER ON THE ROOF
✗✗✗
MINSKOFF THEATRE
200 W. 45TH STREET
SUN JAN 30, 2005 3:00PM

CN 06186
17X
SEC
MEZZ
CA014MIN
J
$ 25.00
J
102

J-TYPE EMG0130M
EVENT CODE

THE MEZZ
C
FRONT MEZZ RICH
NST4013
29FEB00
MUSIC MAN
NO REFUNDS/NO EXCHANGES
NEIL SIMON THEATRE
250 W. 52ND ST, NYC
THU MAY 11, 2000 8:00PM

J-TYPE SPRING
ADM 8
All Taxes Incl. If Applicable

NEDERLANDER

ADMIT ONE SUBJECT TO THE CONDITION ON THE BACK
1342613307 21

Our rescued Puggle, Riley!

AL HIRSCHFELD THEATRE
302 WEST 45TH STREET
MAN OF
LA MANCHA
8:00 PM WED
AUG 27, 2003
RATKT1006 0827 U260Z
*INCL $1 RESTORATION CHG
NOT FOR RESALE

AMBTLM082703E

50%OFF
$48-50 *
BWYEVE TE
MEZZO
M 17

SUBJECT TO TERMS AND CONDITIONS ON REVERSE SIDE.

JB00
21
EVENT CODE
$ 44.50
7.50
SECTION/AISLE
21
VI 64
ZUS708
3MAR0

THE MEZZ
ticketmaster.ticket
SECTION/AISLE   ROW/BOX   SEAT
"GOT MILK?" PRESENTS
BRITNEY SPEARS
ticketmaster
TUE JUNE 27, 2000 7:30PM
JONES BEACH THEATER
NO REF/EX/REC/CAM/BOT/CAM

T 9   ADULT
ADMISSION

VIRGINIA THEATRE
245 WEST 52ND STREET
FLOWER DRUM
SONG
8:00 PM SAT
OCT 19, 2002
KAWEB1128-0824-Y76Y
* THEATRE RESTORATION CHG.
USHKOWITZ, BRAD

AVIRFD
TAMSTR TM
EST. PRICE
95 - 00
1 - 00
TOTAL
96 - 00
ORCHC
P 111

SUBJECT TO TERMS AND CONDITIONS ON REVERSE SIDE

GYPSY2
RMEZ C P 111
$ XXX.XX
PRICE & ALL TAXES INCL
REAR MEZZ CENTER

RMEZ C
CA 13X
P 111
PAL403A
20NOV02

ADULT
All Taxes Incl. If Applicable
ADM 8
BC/EFA PRESENTS
THE 14TH ANNUAL
GYPSY OF THE YEAR
THE PALACE THEATRE
1564 BROADWAY, NYC
TUE DEC 10, 2002 3:00PM

PLAYBILL
WINNER!
BEST MUSICAL

16

My boarding pass for my callback for Glee in LA.

From when I sang the National Anthem at 13 and then at 24.

BOARDING PASS

USHKOWITZ/JENNA

FLIGHT DL 601
DATE 11 SEP
SEAT 12C
ORIGIN NYC-KENNEDY
ZONE 9
DESTINATION LOS ANGELES

OPERATED BY DELTA AIR LINES

RONNY TURIAF
VIP
THE NEW YORK KNICKS
vs. LOS ANGELES LAKERS
FRIDAY, FEBRUARY 11, 2011 at 8:00 PM
GAME KC27
GATE 63
COURTSIDE 11
ROW AA
SEAT 2
PRICE $1745.12
TAX $154.88
TOTAL: $1900.00
USE CLUB ENTRANCE

ALYCWH111104E

LYCEUM THEATRE
149 WEST 45TH STREET NYC
WHOOPI
8:00 PM THU
NOV 11, 2004
MALYC3003-1111-B139Q
*INCLUDES $1.25 FACILITY FEE

STUDNT
$26.25 *
CASH CA
ORCHC
A 103

AMAJPH070102E

MAJESTIC THEATRE
245 W. 44TH ST. N.Y.C.
THE PHANTOM
OF THE OPERA
8:00 PM MON
JUL 1, 2002
MAMAJ1200-0701-J341D
THIS TICKET IS NONREFUNDABLE

55.00
CASH CA
ORCH15
BB 14

Knicks VS. Philadelphia
Friday, Dec 10, 1999
002-5661

JB0627
21
T 11
ADULT
ME22 STAIR 2
"GOT MILK?" PRESENTS
BRITNEY SPEARS
ticketmaster
TUE JUNE 27, 2000 7:30PM
JONES BEACH THEATER
NO REF/EX/REC/CAM/BOT/CAM

SG0211E
TOWER A GATE 70
ADULT ESG0211E
$ 69.50
233
9.20
233
MC 174X
B 12
ZVS704A
B 12
8DEC04
B 12 FC
4.50
CN 26216
233
174X
B
A 69.50
12

JOSH GROBAN***LIVE!
FRIENDSOFJOSHGROBAN.COM
MADISON SQUARE GARDEN
7TH AVE AT 32ND STREET
FRI FEB 11, 2005 8:00PM
ticketmaster
get tickets at ticketmaster.com

PLAYBILL
NEDERLANDER THEATRE

VIRGINIA THEATRE
245 WEST 52ND STREET
LITTLE WOMEN
7:00 PM TUE
JAN 4, 2005
XAWEB1391 0921 W39G
'CL $1 RESTORATION CHG
OWITZ, BRAD

AVIRLW010405E
DMAIL
$65.00 *
TADISC TD
ORCHO
M 6

EUGENE O'NEILL THEATRE
230 W. 49TH ST.
NINE
2:00 PM SUN
NOV 2, 2003
XAWEB1200 1007 Y101U
*INCL $1 RESTORATION CHG
USHKOWITZ, BRAD

AEONNI1
EMLD
$66.00
TAVISA
ORCH
K 18

PLAYBILL
ETHEL BARRYMORE THEATRE

SG1210E
SIDE STAGE GT 72
JRZVIP ESG1210E
$30.00
12.00
313
ZVS713X
310CT04

313
H & M
L 13 FC
4.50
313
L
212X
J 130.00
13

H & M PRESENTS
Z100'S JINGLE BALL 2004
DOORS OPEN AT 6PM
MADISON SQUARE GARDEN
FRI DEC 10, 2004 7:00PM
JBZVIP
CN 51411
212X
ticketmaster
get tickets at ticketmaster.com

My friend Darren Criss (aka Blaine on *Glee*) will tell you I am always scribbling things down. Guilty as charged! I am a jotter/journaler/doodler, and I save *everything*: old Playbills, ticket stubs, birthday cards, photos, finger paintings, you name it. Why? To remind me of where I came from and where I want to go. Some people collect stamps or coins or comic books; I collect moments. Each piece reminds me of a moment in my life that made me more aware of who I am or who I want to be/don't want to be. I collect song lyrics and quotes, too. Stuff that moves me to think and act. Here's a fave:

One of our crew members drew these Valentine's cards. It's vampire Tina!

"HAPPINESS IS FOR THE TAKING . . . AND THE MAKING."
-Oprah

I have a million others (many of which you'll find sprinkled throughout this book). I tend to collect happy, gathering it up around me whenever it presents itself. Being happy attracts happy. If you're happy for long enough, you'll find yourself like a magnet . . . pulling in all the happy people around you, too. You'll find happiness brings upon you ambition, success, love, friendship—all the good stuff! I'm also a collector of advice; when I was younger, they dubbed me "The Little Sponge." So I've asked some of the coolest, smartest people I know: "What is the secret to happiness?" Everyone has their own answers and their own journey. Kevin McHale says, "Happiness, to me, is feeling a rush of inspiration and then getting the chance to act on it," while Kristin Chenoweth believes "The secret to happiness is to simply be myself. It's not always pretty or happy, but I am always ME. I want to live authentically." My best friend from my *Spring Awakening* days, Blake Bashoff, says, "The secret to happiness is to take life as it comes and make the best of it. Keep a positive outlook and move with the flow." I've taken all of their advice to heart, added my own experiences and insights, and forged my own "Happiness Rx"— which in turn, became the beginnings of this book.

The secret to happiness is to simply be myself. It's not always pretty or happy, but I am always ME. I want to live authentically.

"Happiness, to me, is feeling a rush of inspiration and then getting the chance to act on it.

When I tell people I'm writing a book about "choosing glee," they don't seem too surprised. I'm a dork—I don't take myself too seriously, and I smile and giggle a lot, and I laugh way too loud (you can hear me a mile away). Things *do* get me down, but not for too long. I refuse to harp on any situation that makes me sad. What's the use? It's just wasting time and energy. I accept it, have a good cry, and I move on. And it takes a helluva lot to piss me off or freak me out—I'm more of a "whatever will be, will be" kind of girl. I trust the universe knows what it's doing even if I don't. I believe that everything happens for a reason and that every mistake you make brings you closer to the truth. I don't dwell, I don't mope, and I try my damnedest not to hold a grudge. I keep movin' on (like the song goes . . .).

> IT TAKES A HELLUVA LOT TO PISS ME OFF OR FREAK ME OUT— I'M MORE OF A "WHATEVER WILL BE, WILL BE" KIND OF GIRL.

And I'd like to help you do the same. I'm here to be your friend, to share my experiences, and to help you find your way. I'm not going to lecture you or tell you what to do. Instead, you're going to make your own decisions. That's the point. Not one of us is the same or has the same life, heart, or mind. I believe in following what is truly in your heart. You have to figure out what makes you happy. Will you read this book and walk away with ALL the answers? Well, probably not, but you'll look at the world just a little differently than when you started. You'll have hope, faith, and a plan, Stan.

My favorite teacher Mr. H in Holy Trinity Diocesan High School in Hicksville taught me an incredible lesson on hope when we read the play *The Laramie Project*. *Laramie* is a tragic story of a gay man who is beaten to death and the town's reaction to this heinous hate crime. It's based on real interviews with Laramie residents. There's this great line in it: "This whole thing, you see what I'm saying, this whole thing ropes around hope. H-O-P-E." Out of this hate springs forth tolerance, faith, and hope for the future. I never realized how much it resonated when I was that young. Today, I have so many gay friends whom I regard as family. Gay is not a choice; it's a part of who someone is. No one can change or "fix" that. It's like someone telling me to stop being Asian! In the play, the community must move past this horrible act and find hope. I know now that hope is trusting your instincts, having faith in yourself and your journey, and releasing positive energy into the world and believing it will come back to you. Hope is chasing your dreams and standing up for your beliefs.

I have learned that life is what you make of it. I have an amazingly cool, steady job, but I'm still not quite sure what I want to be when I grow up. I like the path life is taking me on, but I want to keep challenging myself. That's the key—I promise you—to long-term happiness: You always have to keep growing. So as I write this book, based on the Ten Rules that have truly transformed my life, I hope we can learn and grow together. I'm still a student of life as well. I'll never stop dreaming or reaching for the stars. There is always more happiness to be had!

This book is for anyone who has ever felt like they are alone or lost, anyone who has hit some hard times and needs a confidence boost, anyone who isn't quite certain what they want to do or be or how to get there. Be you. Be strong. Be positive. There is so much glee in the world if you just look for it.

5 minutes to glee
Get In tune!

At the end of every chapter, you'll see these fast and easy tips for sneaking a little happy into your day. They're my go-to tricks when I need an instant "upper" in my day. Music is a biggie for me. Don't get me wrong—when I'm having a bad day, I'll emo-out and listen to my favorite angsty, sad songs and belt them out to make myself feel better. But mostly my playlists consist of inspirational anthems or songs that lift me up and get me going. Crank it up and dance it/sing it out!

"Stronger" – Kelly Clarkson

"Born This Way" – Lady Gaga

"Blow Me (One Last Kiss)" – Pink

"Charlie Brown" – Coldplay

"Shake It Out" – Florence and the Machine

"Firework" – Katy Perry

"Turn to Stone" – Ingrid Michaelson

"Ours" – Taylor Swift

"Never Going Back Again" – Kevin McHale

"Give Your Heart a Break" – Demi Lovato

FIRM HOLD
AEROSOL FINISHING SPRAY
BRUSHABLE & FAST DRYING

Jenna   Kevin

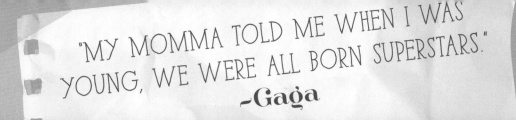

"MY MOMMA TOLD ME WHEN I WAS YOUNG, WE WERE ALL BORN SUPERSTARS."
-Gaga

RULE 1
BE YOURSELF

tina Cohen-Chang is the perfect example of someone who started out with not a clue on how to be true to herself. In the beginning, my character on *Glee* was really confused; she had no idea how to act around people. She wore these crazy Goth clothes so she purposefully wouldn't fit in and formed this fake stutter so people would think she was weird and keep their distance. Then she finally found herself when she found glee club. It was filled with people who were different and embraced their individuality.

The Lady Gaga episode!

"We're d-d-d-doomed" —Tina

Though I can't say I like to wear that much black eyeliner or purple hair extensions, I get where Tina was coming from. When I was in Woodland Middle School on Long Island, I found it a lot easier to be a shape-shifter than to own up to who I truly was. Yup, I was pretty much a doormat up until the eighth grade. I would never speak up, even if I felt something was not right. I knew deep down that making fun of the girl with the mismatched shirt and pants was wrong, but I wanted to fit in so badly . . . it was her or me. I'd also lie about my auditions and voice/dance lessons in the city. If my friends complained that I was never around after school to hang out, I'd blame it on my parents. I was teased because my life wasn't "normal." It wasn't "cool" to not hang around after school, walk home with the clique, or go to movies on a weekend. But most of the time, any hours I had after school were spent pursuing my career. Maybe the kids in school were jealous. But the entire time, I never once owned up to the fact that I loved it. If they made fun of me that I wasn't around, I passed the buck. I said it was my parents who were making me go. (so not true!)

My cool crowd was far from cool: We all wore big Mudd bell-bottom jeans and matching sneakers and hung out at the playground after school or at someone's house. It gave me a sense of belonging, but I felt like a phony. I didn't really fit into this clique; I was just playing a role. They were all already hooking up with boys when their parents weren't home, spraying shaving cream on people's cars on Halloween, and making fun of anyone who wasn't "us."

I was terrified of confrontation, so I never stood up for myself. In middle school, there was a girl (let's call her Caty) who wasn't the most popular person. I got paired up with her for a science project, and I spent a lot of time at her house, and we would have a blast. She was amazing. We had similar tastes in music and movies. We'd collage and scrap book, sing songs, and just have a grand old time. Caty was really smart and extremely talented. When we started to become friends, I knew that the group of friends I normally hung with would not be happy. She wasn't part of the pack. So, whenever they asked why we were hanging out or sitting together at lunch, I'd say it was because of the science project—and would make sure to add that she was "so annoying."

> **I was terrified of confrontation, so I never stood up for myself.**

Then one day I came to school and heard a rumor going around that Caty stuffed her bra with bandanas and tissues and didn't shower. I knew this wasn't true. She walked around school, ignoring the whispers, with her head held high. I was sitting with her at lunch when I suddenly felt something bounce off me; it was a french fry covered in ketchup. They were throwing fries at her and laughing and calling her names. The poor girl continued to sit there and eat her lunch and not say a word or turn around. I didn't say anything, and I didn't stand up for her, even though I knew she didn't deserve to be bullied like that. I wanted to yell, "Stop it! She's an amazing girl!" but instead, I remained silent and kept our friendship a secret. I was too worried what everyone else would think. I was too afraid to confront her to even apologize for the terrible acts that had occurred. I believe Caty forgave me, because we'd have cordial smiles in the hallway when we passed each other but I never quite forgave myself.

broadway baby

You come to a point where you have to ask yourself—do I want to stand out or fade in? Do I want to be who I truly am, or do I want to change myself to fit someone else's idea of right and wrong? For me, that point came along in eighth grade when I became one of the Broadway Kids. I was at a photo-shoot with my friend Chris Trousdale. He had been in *Les Mis* and *The Sound of Music*, and he told me that he belonged to a singing group composed of kids who performed on Broadway. He convinced me that since I was in *The King and I*, I should audition.

Jenna Ushkowitz
AGE: 12
BROADWAY: The King & I
FILM: Babyface

So I went through a private audition, singing "My Favorite Things" from *The Sound of Music* and performing a dance routine they showed me. Before I knew it, I became one of the Broadway Kids. We did two-hour-long shows every week at the John Houseman Theater. We sang songs from Broadway shows, recorded albums, and traveled all over the country. It was an eye-opening experience—and not just because I got to see places like Arizona and Illinois. For the first time in my life, I realized I could just be me—and that was good enough. These kids liked me for who I was, and I didn't have to pretend to be someone I wasn't.

☺

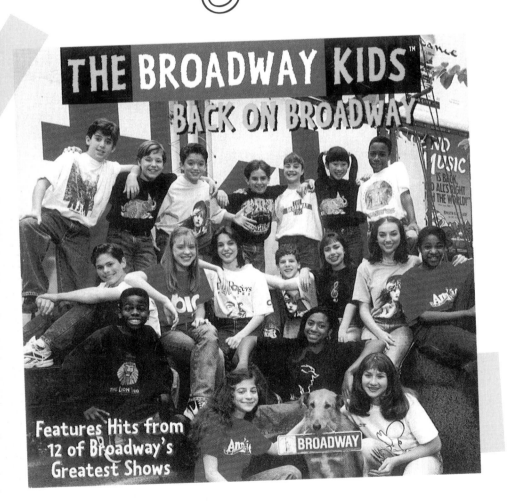

jenna for prez

I came out of the Broadway Kids with so much confidence, and I started over at a new private school, Holy Trinity Diocesan High School, in 2004, away from all the toxic energy of middle school. I was so self-assured, I decided in the end of my freshman year to run for class president. My mom always told me that I was a natural-born leader—time to put it to the test! I remember writing my speech and being terrified I'd get up in front of the assembly and freeze and forget it. I was running against this kid, Ronald, who was really smart. Neither one of us was the coolest, but I thought he could probably outtalk me on the issues.

My new best friend Alexa agreed to run with me as VP. I wasn't going to promise things I couldn't do, like add a waterslide to the yard or make lunch free, but I knew that with a positive attitude, I could handle whatever was needed. We made posters by hand and printed out fliers, and I had to give a speech in front of 450 classmates. And in case you're wondering . . . I won (and remembered every word of that speech)! I still do today and it went something like this: "I can't promise you a pool on the fifth floor or free soda, but what I can promise is my dedication, trust, and honesty to lead you into a great year. I will make sure our student council listens to your concerns with care. I can promise a change that hears the voice of 2004, and a year full of leadership, fun, and most of all ... balance." Not bad, huh?

33

WHEN JENNA MET LEA

When I was doing *The King and I* in 1995, Lea was doing *Les Misérables*. There's a small community of Broadway kids, so there are auditions that every kid is at, and I would see her all the time. We have been friends since then, at the age of nine! Lea came to my birthday parties, like the one for my thirteenth birthday at Jekyll & Hyde Restaurant, and we were always talking on the phone through three-way calling with our mutual friend (my boyfriend at the time), Brandon.

We lost touch when we went to high school, though. I didn't audition as much and she was busy performing in *Fiddler on the Roof*. Then, when I was in college, she landed a role in *Spring Awakening*. After I graduated, I went to see it and loved it. I had heard they were looking for replacements, so I auditioned. I was devastated when I didn't get a role, but when they asked me to come in and read about six months later I got it that time! It was a swing role (a person who covers numerous roles in a show in case one of them can't perform), and I was so excited! (If you wait, good things will come!) Lea brought me in her dressing room, welcomed me, and introduced me to everyone. We were different people, more grown up and mature, but we still reconnected. We were both living the performing life, not just dreaming of breaking into it. We had so much more to talk about. What I admire most about Lea is her determination and her commitment to her own happiness. No matter how busy or stressed she is, she takes time out to breathe. This is something I always strive to do with her finesse. She's never one to sell out or give up, and in this business, that's a rarity.

Lea moved out to LA to do the Hollywood Bowl's *Les Misérables*, and I was still in New York doing *Spring Awakening*. Then I heard, "Lea got the girl, the lead singer, in *Glee*." I texted her and I said, "Hey! I'm auditioning, too! I'm in callbacks." She said, "I KNOW! I HEARD! I'm so excited for you!" Then, I got it too. So our paths just always kept crossing, all these years. I was thrilled when we finally got to work together and sing together in the episode "Props" in Season 3. I am so proud to have witnessed her journey from nine years old till *Glee*. We've watched each other grow up, and that's an incredible bond to share.

Me, Lilli Cooper, and Lea

"Being yourself is the key to true happiness. I've always stuck to who I am, and done what I believe in, and it's always put a smile on my face!"

—LEA MICHELE

breakin' up is (not) so hard to do

Being true to yourself also includes knowing when it's time to move on. Friends come and go, and that's OK. I've learned that people change over time, and you will either grow together or grow apart. Luckily with Lea and me, we have only gotten closer. But when that is not the case, it's best to let go. Some friends will understand that, and you will have a civil parting; other times it can be ugly and dirty. I've had quite a few friends

The A-Listers

who've been jealous and resentful. One particular girl in college had a lot of bad energy. When I stopped hanging out with her, she accused me of dumping her for "The A-listers." But I was able to laugh because it was all so ridiculous. I would never "dump" someone for not furthering my career. She would say things like, "Watch out for Jenna. She wants to hang out with you if you're talented. She'll drop you if you don't help her get a part. . . ." It was hurtful and untruthful because I was never mean to that girl. I had tons of friends from all walks of life, performing and nonperforming, and this was her own insecurity talking. So I walked away from it—and her. Believe me, it wasn't easy, but you learn to weed out the people who can't be happy for you because they're not happy themselves.

CUTTING THE CORD

Once you've decided it's O-V-E-R with a pal, how do you handle it?

Well in middle school, that would have been simple: I would have just sat at another cafeteria table. But we do have to be more mature about this (don't we?)

- **HAVE A TALK—IN PERSON OR OVER THE PHONE.** Keep it short and to the point: "You've done something to upset me, and I can't be your friend right now." Don't allow any follow-up debate or discussion. Leave the room or say good-bye before she begs for forgiveness—or tells you off.

- **WRITE A NOTE OR E-MAIL.** Not the most ballsy approach, but it'll do the trick: "Although we've been friends for five years, I think it's a good idea for us to take a little break. This isn't about you. It's about me needing some space to figure out who I am and what I need right now for myself." (That's called being true to yourself.)

- **BLAME IT ON SOMEONE ELSE.** This is the kinder, gentler way. And it will work if you're desperate. "Sorry, I need to spend time with my mom/sis/ significant other/new pet bunny. . . ."

TINA:

You ignored me for weeks this summer.

ARTIE:

I was playing a marathon game of Halo, woman.

AM I lying to myself?

I know. I know . . . Homework was never my idea of a party, either. I hated it so much that I used to do it in class so that I never had any when I got home. My parents would always ask, "Don't you have homework?" I'd just smile and reply, "Did it!"

So the last thing I want to give you is homework! I want you to think of these exercises (you'll find a few in every chapter) as the work you need to do to find the happiness you want and deserve. They're not homework; they're "heartwork"—so let's call it that. You can't roll up your sleeves, get down to business, and make the life you want until you take some inventory. So pick up that pen or pencil, and start taking stock. Answer TRUE or FALSE to the following statements.

TRUE	FALSE	
☐	☐	I sometimes feel uncomfortable around people who I think are my friends.
☐	☐	I hang out with people who criticize or try to change me.
☐	☐	If I disagree with something someone says, I keep my mouth shut. Why cause trouble?
☐	☐	If I think my friends won't like an outfit, I don't dare wear it—even if I think it's cute.
☐	☐	I would rather follow than lead.
☐	☐	My happiness depends on people liking me.
☐	☐	My success depends on people accepting me.
☐	☐	I sometimes do things just to please others.
☐	☐	I let people make decisions for me.
☐	☐	I have hopes/dreams I don't share with anyone.

If you answered TRUE to any of the above, it's time to take a long, hard look in the mirror. Is this the path you want to be on? Lying to yourself doesn't feel good. If you keep lying to yourself, eventually you'll bury yourself in a land of lies that you won't even be able to keep track of. People know when you're lying. You'll lose valuable people in your life, and you won't be living a truly happy existence. Self-deception is a double whammy: You are lying to yourself, *and* you know it.

➤ Worry about yourself...not everyone else

If you are always comparing yourself to others, you can never truly focus on what's inside of you and what you're capable of achieving. You can't make a plan of action for yourself when you're busy watching what everyone else is up to. For example, on *Glee* everyone is so incredibly talented. If I looked at everyone and said, "Why can't I sing like her?" or "Why can't I dance like him?" it would be a total waste of my time and energy. I'd be holding myself back from my best self.

Remember when I landed a role in *Spring Awakening* on Broadway as a swing? Well, to be honest, instead of being thrilled to have this opportunity, I started thinking that I wasn't special enough to be a star. "That must be why they made me a backup," I told myself. I was forgetting about successes I had already achieved. I was more focused on who got what part instead of what I was doing well. Then one of my producers explained that it takes real skill and talent to cover five different roles and be ready to go on at the drop of a hat. He made me realize how important I was to the show, and I changed my whole outlook. People say the grass is always greener, but you don't have to see it that way. I'm lovin' my own backyard these days. I wouldn't trade what I have and who I am for anything.

JPF, my voice teacher from high school, came to see me on Broadway!

Heartwork Assignment 2

All About Me
↓

Make a list of all the things you like about yourself . . .

Then make a list of the things you don't like . . .

Here's mine . . .

WHAT I LIKE ABOUT ME
(for today):

– I'm being productive with my
  time. (I'm writing this instead of
  flipping channels.)

– I am a good friend and a good
  girlfriend.

– I am responsible and organized.
  (Did anyone see where I put
  my cell phone?)

– I listen, not just speak.

– I can see the big picture and evaluate
  before acting.

– I am patient. (Are we done with this list yet?)

WHAT I DON'T LIKE ABOUT ME (for today)

– I often bite off more than I can chew.

– Sometimes I agonize instead of taking action
  because I hate confrontation.

– I put my phone on "silence" if I just can't deal.

– I'm stubborn.

– It takes a while for me to trust and let people in.

– I still think of exercise as a chore . . . even though I know it's good
  for me.

ch-ch-ch-changes . . .

Change is good. If there is something that needs to be altered in your life, something that is off balance, it means it's time for a change. It may not be the easiest or most wanted, but it can shift your life. I'm a Taurus, so I just naturally, stubbornly resist change. But when I talk myself into accepting change, something pretty magical occurs. This past year, 2012, was a huge transitional phase for me. I moved into a new apartment. The show is evolving. I am developing new things in my career, and my personal life is shifting in a wonderful way. All of these changes made me nervous: Venturing into the unknown is a scary thing. But you need to let your gut be your guide: If something isn't right, you'll feel it in the pit of your stomach. I try to trust the universe and take the leap.

When I first moved out to LA in 2009, I was in shock that I was going so far from home and away from everything and everyone I knew. I found a small apartment to rent through a friend. She had a renovated unit, so when I looked online, I thought mine was renovated, too. Nope. It was cold and dark. It had flickering fluorescent lights that felt like something out of *One Flew Over the Cuckoo's*

"I'M STARTING WITH THE MAN IN THE MIRROR, I'M ASKING HIM TO CHANGE HIS WAYS . . ."
—"Man in the Mirror," Michael Jackson

Nest. I rode up the old rickety elevator with my three suitcases and a few hundred dollars to my name and walked into the frigid, empty apartment. I sat on the toilet and BAWLED. What was I doing? I knew no one, except the friend who had helped me find the place . . . who at the time was a full-time nursing student who had no time for herself, let alone me. I had no sense of direction, and my car hadn't arrived from the East Coast yet. (It was being shipped across country on an

My first apartment in LA—spooky!

eighteen-wheeler.) I almost ran straight back home to my parents, but I summoned my courage and stuck it out. My mom and dad flew out to help me settle in (and make sure I wasn't having a nervous breakdown). But in the end, I was the one who had to make it work. I furnished my place, learned to navigate the freeways, and made lots of great friends. Looking back on it now, it was an amazing experience in forging my independence as an adult. If I could survive those first weeks, I can survive anything.

Change is sometimes thrust upon you whether you like it or not. Season 3 of *Glee* was a year of huge upheaval for all of us. After my family of seniors graduated from the show (Dianna, Harry, Amber, Naya, Chris, Lea), I became uncertain about the future of the show and my part. I didn't know how much of McKinley or Tina viewers would see.

Fortunately, my role has become much more present, and I'm so psyched. But at the same time, I miss my castmates and not being able to hang with them 24/7. These were the people I spent three years with! We went on two concert tours, a mall tour, and an Australian tour together. The set felt eerily empty without them.

I was thrown into a new world with "underclassmen" characters: Ryder, Jake, Kitty, Marley, and Wade/Unique. I was forced to create a new dynamic with these brand-new kids and the actors who play them. In the beginning, I wasn't all that excited about it. So apologies, gang, if I didn't welcome you with open arms right away! I'm a tough nut to crack when it comes to new people. But it didn't take me long to learn how eager, hardworking, and willing these guys were to learn and be the best they can be. It was refreshing. Yeah, I miss the old gang, but I have a whole new extended family now, and I got to explore a great friendship with Vanessa Lengies who plays Sugar Motta. I can't believe that it took me a whole season to realize how amazing she was and what a great pair of kookiness we make together!

I don't know what's going to happen when Tina graduates. But that's the fun of it—allowing the journey to be created in the moment. Yes, I'm beginning to breathe a little heavier. And I'm thinking, "Will I have a job next year?" Maybe, maybe not. But it's a good thing. It keeps me on my toes!

Blake, Heather, Melissa, and I with our director, Adam Shankman...look! We all fit!

SAYING GOOD-BYE TO THE GRADUATES

I relived my experience of graduating high school all over again last year when my friends Dianna, Amber, Harry, Lea, Cory, Chris, and Naya graduated McKinley High. I knew these people would always be a part of my life, but not my *everyday* life—and that felt strange and uneasy.

I remember our choreographer Zach Woodlee came in while "the seniors" were rehearsing to shoot "Music in You" to perform for us "juniors." He said, "just remember this is the last time you'll all be in this choir room singing together."

We all looked at each other with sad faces. It was a bittersweet moment, knowing we were all moving on to something new, fresh, and fun, but also looking into each other's teary eyes and remembering all the incredible times we had together on set and on tour. As we shot that episode, I tried to soak in every moment, knowing that things would never be the same. Time to open a new chapter in our lives.

I miss everyone. It's different on *Glee*. Good, but different. We basically spent every waking moment together for three years. That's a bond that's unlike any other, and only the people who went through it will understand. We are family, and it's hard when you get split up for a bit. Everyone is thriving, doing new, exciting, challenging things and moving upwards and onwards. We're proud and happy for one another, but we also miss what we had. Some experiences are so special they remain forever imprinted on your heart.

"I believe one of the secrets that brings me happiness is acceptance. When I accept things the way they are, I can relax from trying to force life and simply enjoy the ride and see the beauty in every unique moment. Another secret is my friends (like a certain 'Unna Jshkowitz'). And also cupcakes!"

—Vanessa Lengies

what you can/can't change

There are lots of things you can't change in life. You can't change your past; what's done is done. You can't change certain situations. Some people make lots of plans, and fate throws a curveball. You can't change the day of the week or the weather. And you can't change other people. Believe me, I've tried, and it doesn't work. You don't get to "fix" people—that's their job, not yours. It's a waste of time wishing that people around us were different; that they would stop or start doing something, that they would grow up, wise up, and move on.

What you can change is how you act, feel, and relate. You can change how you treat yourself and others. You can change your attitude and your priorities. You can change your name: Lady Gaga—Stefani Germanotta, and Lea Michele— Lea Michele Safarti. I guess I could have been "Lady Jenna" if I wanted. Or maybe Jenna Noelle? (Noelle is my middle name.) God knows, tons of producers and casting agents advised me to lose "Ushkowitz." In show business, you don't want a last name that's going to pigeonhole you into the same roles. In my case, I walked in the door and I was already "The Asian Jew." Even now, many an audition starts with, "Soooo, USHKOWITZ . . . where did *that* name come from?" I don't mind. It's always good to leave them with

"SHOULD I GIVE UP OR SHOULD I JUST KEEP CHASING PAVEMENTS?"
—"Chasing Pavements," Adele

47

something to remember you by, right? Besides, I had a ton of other changes I needed to go through first (and probably still do!). To discover who you truly are, I firmly believe you need to rock the boat and shake things up a little. People sometimes misinterpret "being yourself" as staying put/stuck/super-glued to a situation that's not working. A butterfly starts out as a caterpillar; sometimes you start out as one thing and grow into another.

The family at Christmas, 2011

5 REASONS CHANGE IS A GOOD THING

1. If you stand still for too long, it gets pretty boring and your feet will hurt. Being yourself doesn't always mean being the same self. Life changes. It moves pretty fast, and you have to move with it. There are things about you that you should never compromise (your integrity, your passion, your beliefs). Think of the things that you wish were different or better—this is where it's okay to make some shifts.

2. Change is growing. The more new things you confront, the more experience you gather. I never spoke Korean, but thanks to taking on the lyrics for the "Gangnam Style" song on *Glee*, I'm ready to take on my next PSY song!

3. Change makes you wiser for the next time around. If things never changed, you wouldn't learn anything. I stayed too long in a crappy relationship because I was scared to let go. Now I know that I can stand on my own two feet. It also showed me what I want/don't want in a boyfriend. Now I found someone who loves me for me.

4. Change is a friendly reminder that nothing is impossible. You feel so accomplished once you get through the hard part. For me, learning to eat right and exercise was a huge challenge. Me? Get up at the crack of dawn to work out? Are you kidding? But I did. I powered through it. And now I not only look better, I feel better.

5. Change brings opportunity, adventure, and excitement. If you don't welcome it, you're closing a door you barely opened. If I didn't welcome the "new New Directions" and try to get to know them all, I'd be missing out on an awesome season, a lot of laughs and great new friends.

do I need a change in my life?

Often we know deep down that we need to change and grow. No matter how old you are—or how tall you are—you should always strive to keep evolving. Challenge yourself to be better, stronger, healthier, happier.

Before you say, "Nah, everything's fine . . . ," answer the following honestly:

- *Are you tired?*
- *Are you pissed off?*
- *Are you stressed?*
- *Are you embarrassed?*
- *Are you bored?*
- *Are you sad?*
- *Are you desperate?*
- *Are you resentful?*
- *Are you unsure?*
- *Are you looking for a way out?*

If you answered YES to any of the above, it may be time to shake things up. To achieve a new phase in your life doesn't take luck or circumstance. It takes action. It takes support—real friends and family who believe in you and will be there to catch you should you fall. It takes asking for help if you need it. (How many times have I asked Heather or Harry—dancing machines—to run me through a step one more time if I'm off count?) But above all, it takes faith in yourself that there is a better option out there if you seek it. You have to find the motivation to walk the path. I'm not going to drag you; no one is. That kick in the ass you need has to come from within. Comfortable is safe, but it's not exciting.

5 minutes to glee
Connect online with a friend

I'll admit it—I'm addicted to social media. I tweet; I post; I blog. But I think it's all a great way to stay in touch with my friends and fans. If you need a quick boost or a time-out in a hectic day, spend just five minutes messaging someone you miss or reading what your friends are up to on Facebook. I always find something that makes me smile—like Lea posting a pic of herself as Little Cosette (I remember her that way!) or Kristin Chenoweth tweeting a pic of her sweet puppy giving her a smooch.

Jenna Ushkowitz @JennaUshkowitz
"On a bright cloud of music shall we fly?" :) loved hearing 'Shall We Dance' throughout Iron Lady movie. Brought me back to my 9 yr old self.

Jenna Ushkowitz @JennaUshkowitz
Is it just me, or does doing nothing feel more productive when you're doing nothing with someone else?

Jenna Ushkowitz @JennaUshkowitz
"For attractive lips, speak words of kindness. For lovely eyes, seek out the good in people…" -Audrey Hepburn

Jenna Ushkowitz @JennaUshkowitz
Not having a working phone is weirdly liberating and the most terrifying thing all at the same time…

Jenna Ushkowitz @JennaUshkowitz
The conversations you hear in waiting rooms are gold. Pure gold.

Jenna Ushkowitz @JennaUshkowitz
Those Google Chrome commercials make me teary!

Jenna Ushkowitz @JennaUshkowitz
"I'm just the same as I was oh don't you understand I'm never changin' who I am." #imaginedragons

We faked it! Lea and I tweeted this pic out warning kids never to text and drive.

RULE 2
KNOW WHAT YOU WANT

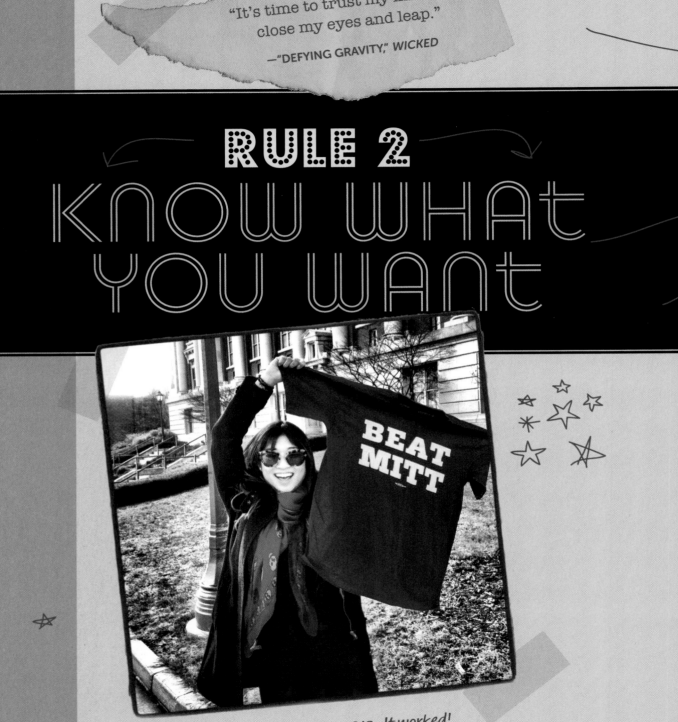

Me campaigning for Obama 2012. It worked!

Getting my 16th tattoo!

You have to know your heart's desire. This might sound silly, because what I really want right now is a burrito (my culinary weakness). But I mean it: Do not allow yourself to live in Shoulda-Coulda-Woulda-Land. It sucks. It feels shaky and unstable all the time, like walking a tightrope. And it keeps you from living in the moment. You need steady ground under your feet; you need a foundation that's rock solid. You need something to hold tight to when things take an unpredictable turn. I've always had goals—but not always the same goal.

When I was little, I wanted to be a veterinarian. I just loved animals and thought it would be fun. In high school, I realized my true calling was performing. Your goals can always change, but you need to have a purpose and your sights set on *something*. It's like circling a place on a map and walking toward that spot because you know it's where you want to be.

Becca Tobin, who plays Kitty on *Glee*, told me she realized when she was four years old that she loved singing and dancing. "I used to watch the movie *Annie* over and over and over, and I would reenact every scene and song. Then my parents took me to see a Broadway show when I was a little older, and at that point I was positive that I wanted to be an actress when I grew up."

Becca Tobin and I at the Sadie Hawkins Dance

Life is filled with possibilities, and settling on just one or two can be tough. Brainstorming is a tool to help you focus on what you really want. It allows you to gather your thoughts and explore them. Lots of people brainstorm out loud every day or while they meditate/daydream. Some pin up photos or quotes on their fridge or a vision board. I make lists—lots and lots of lists. I make a vision board in my head of a few of the goals I want to work toward, then I put them in order of priority. I think about what the best way is to tackle them at this time and what will make me the happiest. There has to be something that makes you want to jump out of bed in the morning and do a happy dance. What is it? If you can't answer that question, then think back to a time in your life when you were your happiest. I have lots of those moments, and they all revolve around being onstage. So that's how I know where my heart lies. I gotta perform!

Finn:
"Tina, what are you good at?"

Tina:
"I-I..."

Finn:
"We'll figure something out for you."

The Original Six!

BRAINSTORMING 101

Sometimes I am stumped. It can be on how to interpret a scene. It can be on what to write for this chapter. It can be what flavor ice cream I feel like eating. The point is, there will be plenty of times and places where your brain just gets stuck—kind of like the home button on your iPhone. If it's not working, nothing is working. Your entire world is on lock down. That's when you need to get the gears running smoothly again and brainstorm!

Set aside a quiet time and place where you can just be inside your head. No distractions. No cell phones. No Facebook. . . .

At the White House, feeling very patriotic.

GIVE YOURSELF A TIME LIMIT—I like to spend about thirty minutes brainstorming, usually at bedtime when I'm done with my work for the day and my mind is less stressed.

CHALLENGE YOURSELF TO THINK BIG! What would be an exciting new thing for you to do? Don't allow your situation/money/time to hold you back. This is a wish list, so wish for the stars.

WRITE DOWN WORDS/IDEAS THAT COME TO YOU. Nothing is stupid or irrelevant. Let your creative juices flow.

LOOK OVER WHAT YOU'VE WRITTEN DOWN AND CHOOSE FIVE IDEAS YOU LIKE THE BEST. What strikes a chord? What makes you smile or your heart beat a little faster?

ONCE YOU KNOW WHAT YOU WANT TO DO, THEN BUILD A ROAD MAP TO MAKE IT HAPPEN. What tools/skills/help do you need to make this dream a reality? How long will it take?

being decisive

There are a lot of options out there—sometimes an overwhelming amount. My job on *Glee* brings me opportunities that pop up when I least expect them. A few weeks ago, I was planning a trip to visit my boyfriend Michael in Atlanta for two days. A movie audition came up, as well as a great opportunity to sing at a charity event. I sat there frozen with indecision. What should I do? I knew Michael would understand, but I also felt guilty. After a reassuring phone call from my man ("You should do it!"), I rescheduled my flight. Then the following week, another audition popped up. This time, I decided to give myself a break and spend some quality time with my very considerate, very patient boyfriend. I was working twelve-hour days all week, and downtime sounded awesome. It was the right choice, because it's what I needed at that moment.

So how can you make a choice about a career, a relationship, or even what you want for dinner? Consider the following:

Do something. The only bad decision is inaction. Don't let an abundance of options paralyze you. Even if you choose wrong, there's something valuable to be learned.

Set a deadline: "You have till tomorrow to make up your mind about this." Otherwise, it's like studying chess pieces on a board and never making your move. You'll never win that way!

Trust your gut. What is it telling you? Let your instincts guide your choices when your brain doesn't know what to do.

Break down the biggies. The life-changing decisions you need to make, like starting a new career, can seem daunting. The trick is to break them down and tackle them one at a time. For example, write down a plan for what you need to do to make it happen: college courses, an internship, looking for employment. Make smaller decisions about each phase of your plan—e.g., What's the best college for this degree? What courses should I take?

Toss a coin. Seriously, if you really are 50/50 on a decision and both are good options, then heads or tails is a great way to make the choice for you.

You can always change your mind. This makes any decision easier to make. If you decide something and it really doesn't work, you can simply try again. I always ask myself, "What's the worst thing that could happen if I make this choice and it's not the right one? Can I live with that fallout?" If yes, then I go for it!

"The secret to happiness is identifying what you're passionate about and being able to do it well everyday. Also surround yourself with a great group of people you love. Laugh, live, and look forward to the future."

—NAYA RIVERA

What am I good at?

What talents do you have? What passions do you want to pursue? Don't limit yourself if they're not particularly practical. Sure, my parents would have been thrilled if I went to medical school, but I always liked to perform. I was in summer theater camp since I was in the second grade, and I took dance, gymnastics, and voice lessons on the side. I was lucky that my profession chose me at a young age. When I was cast in *The King and I* on Broadway at nine years old, I realized that there was nothing that made me happier than being onstage. The things you do best that bring you the greatest satisfaction and joy hold the key to your success. Ask yourself:

What makes me smile, laugh, dance, sing?

What lifts me up?

Who inspires me (celebrities, mentors, historical figures, etc.)?
What is it about this person and their journey that resonates with me?

What am I good at/most proud of?

What makes me special/unique/different?

They had to tape the bubbles together because they would make so much sound during scenes.

« I love wearing champagne bubbles — I get to express a whole different side of myself. Because even though I'm painfully shy and obsessed with death, I'm a really effervescent person...."

—Tina, "Theatricality" Episode

my idol: gaga

Lady Gaga is a huge inspiration and role model for me. She's a true artist; her videos are not music videos—they are short films that inspire her fans. I respect her work and now her work ethic. Being a part of her video for "Marry the Night" was probably one of the most thrilling experiences of my life. Being able to watch her direct and take command of a set was surreal.

Before I had met and hung out with Gaga, I was a huge fan. I'd performed her songs on *Glee*, and I loved her music and her integrity. I've never met someone more committed to her fans. It wasn't a huge surprise to me that she is truly just a twenty-five-year-old woman who has hauled her ass for an amazing career. We had a great connection from the beginning. When we hung out, we talked about girly things and hilariously perverted things and laughed and had a great time.

When I got on the set, she brought me over and introduced me to her friends and everyone working on

Michael and Gaga's awesome kicks.

> When we hung out, we talked about girly things and hilariously perverted things and laughed and had a great time.

61

the shoot. Watching her direct and act was mind blowing. She knows exactly what she wants and really trusts the team she surrounds herself with. She was so focused and professional. She had to wear two hats: run a set and tell a story that was so emotionally raw. In my scene, I had to pretend to be her best friend and 98 percent of it was improv. She taught me to be braver, to commit fully to the moment, to not be afraid to take the leap. I felt accomplished and challenged when we wrapped at 6:00 a.m. I am—and always will be—in awe of Gaga.

try it—you'll like it

Some people love to experience things they've never tried before. They'll order a Pop Rocks Martini (yeah, they exist!) or sample chocolate-covered cockroaches without batting an eyelash. These are the folks that belong on *Fear Factor*! They don't let anything—not tradition, not routine, not the unknown—hold them back from being bold and curious. I, on the other hand, frequent the same few restaurants and have had the same best friends for years and years. I tend to dip

my toe in the water first before I dive in—but I do eventually make a splash. I understand the way it goes: Routine is safe, while unfamiliarity sets off warning bells. But trying something new opens you up to so many great possibilities: you might love it; you might be good at it; you might grow from it. Case in point, my pal Harry Shum, aka Mike on *Glee*. He is one of the hardest workers I've ever known—not to mention one of the greatest dancers. But when it came to doing the number "Dream a Little Dream" on the "Dream On" episode, he was suddenly faced with a huge challenge. He never learned how to tap dance, and we had to do a sweet, old-fashioned, soft-shoe routine. This was way out of his comfort zone. From all my Broadway training, I can handle tap, so it wasn't an issue for me. But Harry was entering uncharted territory. Every minute we weren't filming, he'd be somewhere, working on his moves. He embraced the challenge rather than shying away from it. And in the end, he discovered he's actually a pretty smooth tap dancer! The point is, you never know what you can do till you give it a whirl.

YOU NEVER KNOW WHAT YOU CAN DO TILL YOU GIVE IT A WHIRL.

Harry and I on set rehearsing for our soft shoe number.

65

EXPERIMENT!

We are be-ings—so get out there and be. Do something—don't just contemplate it. Try something so you know what it would feel like if you did it for real. Let it inspire you in a brave, new direction. The more new things you try, the more self-confident you become.

Why don't you . . .

Visit a new place/culture and imagine what it would be like to live there.

Read a book about something you are curious about.

Take a class in something that looks fun or challenging to prove to yourself that you can do it. Always wanted to speak Swahili? Do it!

Invite an acquaintance to lunch or dinner to learn more about what they do/think.

Flex your creative muscles—write a poem, paint a portrait, sculpt a pot—anything that allows you to express yourself in an exciting new way.

Play a new sport for the fun of it; test your physical limitations. (You'll be surprised at how strong you really are!)

Eat in a new restaurant—experiment with new dishes and flavors—or whip up a gourmet meal from a recipe you've always wanted to try.

Buy a ticket to a play, a ballet, an opera—any art form you've never embraced.

Try on a new style—maybe a cool trend you've seen in a magazine. How does it make you feel to wear neon jeans?

Jess and I attached at the hip as usual.

"You will never really know who you are until you make mistakes. . . . Learn from them, but always do what feels right, not what others say is right! In your heart you will always know what's right. And that is all that matters. . . ."

—Jessica Szohr

loving the body you're in

Happiness stems from being content with who you are. There was a time, not so long ago, when I wasn't. Ever since high school, I've had hips and boobs, and my weight has fluctuated. I didn't understand what foods made me gain weight, what foods made me feel sluggish, and what foods were good for me. And as result, I packed on a little more pounds than I wanted, and I felt "soft."

When I first got to LA and saw myself on screen, I freaked out. The cameras made me look bigger than I really was. I figured to look "normal" on camera, I'd have to be a rail. I tried diet pills and starvation—only two granola bars a day and Lean Cuisine at night. I worked out constantly till I was exhausted, hungry, and an emotional wreck. I knew what I was doing to lose weight wasn't okay. It made me feel like crap, not healthy. I worried I was developing an eating disorder, and I knew that was a dangerous road to go down. When we filmed the scenes with Marley starving herself on *Glee* this season, it really took me back to this place. So many young women don't realize how much they're hurting themselves. Marley had to literally fall down and smack her head to knock some sense into her!

Thankfully, I had a minirevelation before reaching that point. I started making healthier choices. I ate three square meals a day—and not just granola bars. Real food: proteins, veggies, and fruit. I even tried being a vegetarian, but my body

Best hot dog from Yankee Stadium.

starting craving meat so I had to listen to it.

Amber likes to keep me in check.

Just as I was starting to get in shape, *Seventeen* magazine called and said they wanted me to help launch their new fitness section. Me? A fitness shoot? I loved to run and do yoga, but this required me to look toned and taut and pose in skimpy workout clothes. I hung up the phone with *Seventeen* and got on the horn right away with a trainer!

I knew the workout would be hard and rigorous, and I wasn't sure how much I would (or could!) be pushed. I was never very secure about my body, and I didn't love the idea of somebody watching me sweat. But it turns out, it was one of the best things I've ever done. My trainer Adam keeps me disciplined while he educates me on nutrition. I'm so glad I did it. I work out with him at least three times a week, and he switches it up so I don't get bored. We'll do drills, weights, and cardio, and I love vinyasa yoga. If you don't have a trainer (or don't wanna pay for one), get yourself a walking/running/exercising buddy. All you need is a person to cheer you on and help motivate you.

Craft Services at work. Yumm.

When it was time for the *Seventeen* shoot I was not just prepared, I was thrilled to show off my fab abs in a crop top! I dropped the extra weight and toned up. I look and feel healthy. And most importantly, I vowed never to weigh myself again and make myself crazy. I know now it's how you feel and not what the scale says that matters.

Sun Salutation

This yoga routine makes me instantly happy and energized. Vinyasa yoga flows from one posture into another, so your body is moving, and your blood is flowing. I love the idea of greeting the sun and embracing a brand-new day.

POSE 1
MOUNTAIN POSE

- Stand with your feet together.
- Hold your arms in a prayer position in front of your chest (palms and fingers touching).
- Lift your toes off the floor and bring them back down again.
- Stretch your head toward the ceiling.
- Draw in your stomach and pull your shoulders down. They should be aligned with your hips.

POSE 2
RAISED HAND POSE

- Now lift your arms to the sides and up.
- Press your palms together over your head.
- Arch your back and look up at your hands.

POSE 3
STANDING FORWARD BEND

- Now bend forward at the hips with your arms out to the sides.
- Bring your hands in front of your feet and try to press your palms to the floor.
- Shift your weight toward the balls of your feet, keeping your hips in line with your ankles. Let your head drop down.

POSE 4
DOWNWARD FACING DOG

- Drop down onto your hands and knees.
- Push up with your toes and straighten your legs.
- Press back with your hands, pushing your butt toward the ceiling.
- Let your head hang down.
- Now shift your weight back to your heels and come forward into a push-up position.
- Press your hips to the floor.
- Arch your back and gaze up toward the ceiling.

70

You can repeat this series several times, quickening your pace as you get more comfortable with the poses.

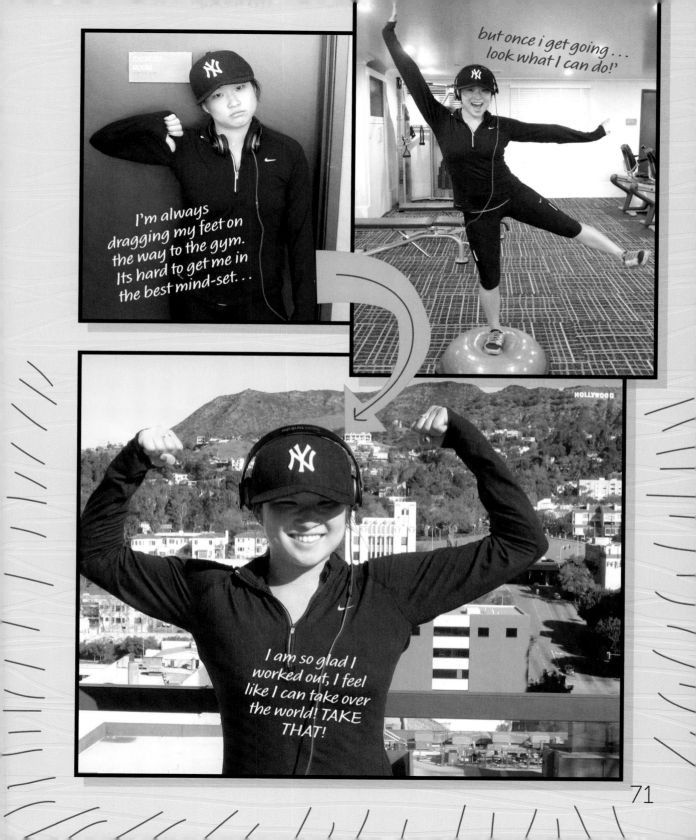

71

motivate yourself to move

Experts will tell you (and I believe them!) that exercise can actually make you happier. Within just thirty minutes of exercise, your body starts to release chemicals called endorphins. These chemicals induce feelings of pleasure and euphoria—kind of like the way you feel when you're in love or you find out you're nominated for an Emmy. (Oh, wait! That's my euphoria!) Knowing that should be enough to get you into the gym for a half hour a day. But in case you still need a little push:

Schedule it in. My biggest excuse when I don't feel like exercising is, "I'm too busy." You're NEVER too busy to sneak in a five-minute walk or to take the stairs instead of the elevator. Make an appointment every day on your calendar to do something physical.

Make it fun. Try not to think of exercise as a chore. Bike with a friend to the mall (and reward yourself shopping!); toss a ball with your dog in the park; go to a club and bust some moves. Guess what? All are great exercise!

Picture yourself slammin' hot. Close your eyes and see *People*'s "Sexiest Man/Woman Alive" cover starring YOU. Exercise can completely transform your body.

Read fitness magazines. They always motivate me. All those people eating healthy and demonstrating squats and crunches. Maybe it's guilt, but I usually run to the gym right after!

72

Chart your progress. As I said, I don't like to measure my progress in numbers; I base it instead on how I feel. But for some people, seeing yourself change is very motivating. If you're one of those types, then by all means, keep a journal, a chart, or a blog. As you see the pounds and inches drop off you'll be inspired to keep up the good work.

Reward yourself. I don't mean eat a box of Oreos after every workout. Make yourself work for that prize! For example, if you drop a whole size (about 10 pounds), treat yourself to a cute new outfit.

Revel in the feeling. After a workout, I'm totally pumped. My adrenaline is rushing; my muscles are burning; and my stress has magically melted away. Take a few minutes to soak that in. Remembering how good it feels will make you crave exercise again tomorrow!

Get a cheerleader. Not the Dallas Cowboys variety—I mean someone who will stand by your side while you sweat. It can be a personal trainer (mine won't take no for an answer!) or a friend who is willing to work out with you. A little pep talk goes a long way.

Keep your eyes on the prize. Think of everything you will get out of this: compliments from co-workers ("Damn, Jenna, you are looking gooood!"); more energy and less aches and pains; a longer life; revenge at your high school reunion (when everyone gained twenty pounds, you lost it!).

it's a plan, man: how to set your goals and stick to them

When I went to college, I made a plan: I was going to graduate in three years. All my friends were a year older, and I wanted to graduate with them. It was so much work! I almost dropped out several times because I just wanted to be done with it. I felt like my head was going to explode! It was extremely difficult to balance my life auditioning and take all those courses. My parents and my roommate/best friend Matty tried to cheer me on. I kept saying to myself, "I've already come this far. I can't turn back now." I dug my heels in (that's the Taurus in me, again!) and refused to let it go. I didn't want anyone—including myself—to think of me as a quitter. I went to my counselor and said, "I want to finish in three years—even if it kills me!" It almost did. I took on more than twenty-one credits a semester including online courses and winter classes. But it was worth it: I completed all my requirements a year ahead of schedule. I walked out those doors with my diploma.

It's easy to be excited about a plan at the start: It's like having the newest iPhone. But after a while, there's a new version, and you're itching to move on to the next one. The trick is to see the bigger purpose behind the goal: What makes it worth sticking to? What makes the sacrifice worth it?

> It's easy to be excited about a plan at the start: It's like having the newest iPhone.

Committing is not easy. Whether you want to lose weight, run a marathon, or (in my case) get a college degree, each of these goals takes an enormous amount of dedication and drive. Life gets in the way. Things happen to distract or deter you. That's when you have to ask yourself, "How bad do I want it?" Anticipate the obstacles. Deal with the setbacks. If one path doesn't get you there, then try another. Just don't ever lose sight of what you really want.

JANE LYNCH, THE TOUGHEST CHICK I KNOW

Coach Sue's got nothin' on her! Jane has been through so much to get where she is in her personal life and in the industry. It took her years and years (about twenty-five!) to become a successful actress, and she's finally getting the recognition she deserves. Jane didn't start out a star; she paid her dues. (She even did a Frosted Flakes commercial!) She has worked in theater groups, written her own one-woman show, and guest-starred in numerous TV shows and movies. She has had her ups and downs, yet she always makes such strong choices. I am so inspired by her ambition, drive, and fervor. She never gives up, and being around such a great actor (and person) pushes me to be a better one.

breaking bad habits

I'm not talking about biting your nails or twirling your hair. I'm talking about things you do that stand in your own way, that defeat your purpose or destroy your self-esteem. FYI, it takes thirty days for a habit to form. So if you do something—or stop doing something—for just a month, you're now conditioned for this behavior.

Kevin and I glued to a computer game. Maybe we need to spend less time at his computer!

I used to be the queen of bad habits. When I was in school, I would always stall and procrastinate—until I realized I was just making everything harder on myself. How could I possibly get a term paper done in two hours? Why had I waited till the very last minute to study for my final exam?

Today, my bad habit is also related to laziness! I tend to cancel plans last minute. Sometimes I'd rather sit on my couch in my pj's and watch TV than go out—even if I made a date with a friend. Sometimes I'd rather take a nap than return a phone call. But I'm working on it! I'm trying to be more social and responsive! I'll turn off the TV and make myself throw on a pair of jeans and go! My friend called the other night and invited me to an event, and I didn't hem and haw or hesitate. I said yes right away, and I went. You know what? I had a great time—much better time than sitting around on my butt, stuffing my face with popcorn.

So how do you kick these self-sabotaging habits to the curb?

Be aware. Notice when you're doing it, what triggers the habit and what feelings are attached to it. That way you can figure out why you're doing it and be able to stop.

Keep a log of when you do it—what time of the day? What were you doing at that moment? Then analyze what might be triggering it: boredom, anxiety, work or school-related stress, et cetera.

Replace it with a better choice. The idea is to channel your energy into something positive. What is a better way to cope with stress? Instead of procrastinating till the last minute, can you set aside ten minutes every day to work on a project? Practice this new habit for thirty days, and it will become second nature to you.

Gimmie, Gimmie

Make a list of ten things you think you want—they could be anything from tangible, concrete things to idealistic goals. Consider why you want them and what the result could be if you get them.

1.

2.

3.

4.

5.

6.

7.

8.

9.

10.

Now I want you to look at all those things you've written down. If a new car, nose job, and a winning lottery ticket were on your list, consider the deeper meaning behind them. "Why do I want those things? What do I hope will be true if I have it (the cool car, money, plastic surgery, etc.)?" Dig a little deeper—what do these things grant you? Freedom? Self-esteem? Security? Success? These are the bigger picture goals you need to be pursuing.

Jenna's List

I want...

1. To direct (TV, movies, music videos)

2. An apartment in NYC

3. There to be a world without war and senseless violence

4. News that isn't led by a celebrity who cheated on another celeb.

5. The perfect comforter for my bed

6. A new pair of Jimmy Choo's

7. Longer legs

8. A lifetime supply of burritos

9. A personal chef

10. An end to poverty

I can see clearly now . . .

Sometimes, I get a bit fuzzy, but I try. I know, for example, that clarity comes from knowing my priorities. If I'm between going to a red carpet event or celebrating my bro's birthday, family always wins out. That decision is crystal clear.

How do you find clarity? Start by making the effort:

Clarity is a decision. It's not something that just lands on your doorstep. You choose it.

Clarity is seeing things with an open and nonjudgmental mind. It is taking a step back and looking at the big picture.

Clarity is asking yourself, "Is this worth getting upset over?" Or "Is this worth fighting for?"

Clarity comes when you put yourself in someone else's shoes and understand why he/she acted the way he/she did.

Clarity is taking the leap in order to get to a place that you haven't been before. It's allowing you to see things in a new light. It's letting go of your inhibitions and letting yourself truly feel.

Clarity can be anything that puts you in a place of peace. I find clarity when things fall into place—when I realize something that made me upset or a situation that didn't work out in the past was necessary to get me to the place I'm in now.

Clarity allows us to love more, breathe stronger, feel deeper. It puts everything into perspective.

clarity

Free your mind

Sometimes, I feel like my thoughts are a big hot mess. I've got so much going on simultaneously that it's impossible to focus. There's way too much noise. That's when you need to do a little spring cleaning: declutter your thoughts, and you'll find you're able to see things for what they truly are. Do these three things today to bring yourself back to a good place:

BE STILL.
By this I mean take ten minutes out of your day to just hide under the covers, curl up in a chair, or close your eyes and be in the moment. Don't let worries about tomorrow or yesterday creep into your thoughts. Just stay in the here and now.

STOP AND SMELL THE ROSES.
Appreciate the little things: a beautiful sunset, the sound of rain hitting your windows, the smell of cookies baking in the oven. Take note and smile.

MAKE A CHOICE—EVEN A SMALL ONE.
Have oatmeal for breakfast instead of a bagel; program your TIVO; book a mani-pedi for the weekend. The act of taking control will calm and reassure you.

SHOULD I OR SHOULDN'T I?

**Life is filled with tough choices and lots of paths you can take.
Before you decide to do something risky, ask yourself:**

→ **Is this a risk worth taking? Why?**

→ **Does it bring me closer to my goals?**

→ **What can I gain?**

→ **What can I lose?**

→ **What is the probable result?**

→ **Will taking this risk hurt myself or others?**

83

5 FOODS THAT CAN MAKE YOU HAPPY

TURKEY: Next time you're in a deli, order up a turkey club. It contains high amounts of phenylalanine, an essential amino acid the brain uses to create dopamine, a neurotransmitter that activates several of the mind's pleasure centers. Translation: gobble some up if you want to feel good.

SALMON: Oily fish like this, as well as tuna, trout, and mackerel, are rich in omega-3 fatty acids. Some studies say these oils are just as effective as antidepressants! They're also good for getting rid of insomnia and boosting your libido. Oh, joy!

SPINACH: Leafy greens are high in folate, which creates serotonin in the brain (a neurotransmitter linked to happy thoughts). Have a spinach salad or chop it up in an omelet for an instant mood boost!

BRAZIL NUTS: They are rich in selenium, a little mineral that keeps depression at bay. Another plus: It's thought to ward off heart disease and cancer (that makes me happy!)

CHOCOLATE: This one's a no brainer. Anyone who's ever eaten a tub of chocolate frosting will tell you there's a lot of truth to this. Chocolate contains cannabinoids, which FYI, are also found in marijuana. So besides the "high" you get from all that sugar, it also has a relaxing effect. Take a few ounces of organic, sweetened, dark chocolate and call me in the morning!

Get COOKIN'

There is something very soothing and comforting about preparing a simple dish for yourself or someone else. The chopping, mashing, and mixing of ingredients makes my anxiety melt away because I'm forced to focus and slow down. It's also a great pick-me-up when all you do is order in Chinese or do takeout from Taco Bell. I love the smell of something on the stove or in the oven.

Jenna's 5-minute chicken burrito

Top a whole-wheat or flour tortilla with $1/2$ cup of grilled chicken, $1/3$ cup of corn, and $1/4$ cup Mexican shredded cheese. Pop in the microwave for 45 seconds. Add salsa and hot sauce and roll up.

RULE 3
"FEAR" IS not the F WORD

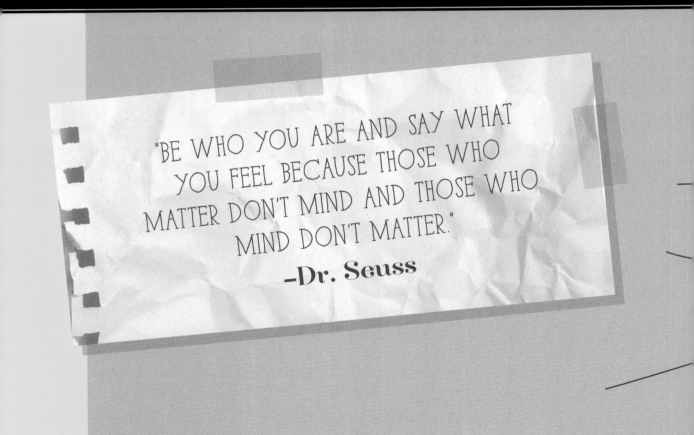

"BE WHO YOU ARE AND SAY WHAT YOU FEEL BECAUSE THOSE WHO MATTER DON'T MIND AND THOSE WHO MIND DON'T MATTER."

–Dr. Seuss

i remember this acting exercise I had to do in improv class once—it's the classic mime where you imagine yourself in a box. Most of my classmates thought it was fun; I found it utterly frustrating and a little freaky. Who wants to feel trapped or boxed in? Yet this is what fear does to you. It puts up walls so you can't move or see a way out. Most of the obstacles I've struggled with in my life have stemmed from fear:

◉ Fear of rejection

◉ Fear of failure

◉ Fear of not being good enough

◉ Fear of losing someone

◉ Fear of change

◉ Fear of the unknown

◉ Fear of being hurt

"Change the voices in your head / Make them like you instead . . ."

—"F***IN' PERFECT," PINK

But fear is something you can/should face. Getting out of your comfort zone, as scary as that may be, is the first step toward accomplishing your goals. The best, strongest, smartest people feel fear. They embrace it. When something scares the crap out of me these days, I ask myself why. What is it that is making me feel uncomfortable, uncertain, or unable to move? Push through and past that fear; know that something even better is waiting on the other side.

READY, SET, BREATHE

This is one of my fave exercises for when I'm scared to death. If you do it a couple of times, it slows down your heart and calms your mind. I even have a tattoo on my finger to remind me.

STEP 1. Suck air in through your nose deeply.

STEP 2. Hold the breath for a few seconds.

STEP 3. Breathe in your nose and exhale slowly but forcefully out of your mouth like you're whistling. Repeat several times.

When I'm nervous, I have to reason with myself. If you let nerves get the best of you, you lose. I don't like to lose. I'm actually a sore loser. So, instead, I always say to myself, "What's the point? Why are you nervous right now? You're gonna get this or you're not, but if you're nervous and jumbly and that makes you screw it up . . . you're really NOT going to get it." Then, I take a deep breath and do what one of my voice coaches taught me. I say in my mind, "F___ you. F___ you. F___ you!!" It puts me back in control.

Sometimes the voice inside your head sounds a lot like Coach Sue: "You can't do it! You're going to screw it up! You don't have what it takes." I say tell it to back off. Take a hike; find someone else's head to screw with.

Unfortunately, it doesn't always listen! I got asked to sing the national anthem at the New York Jets' home opener this

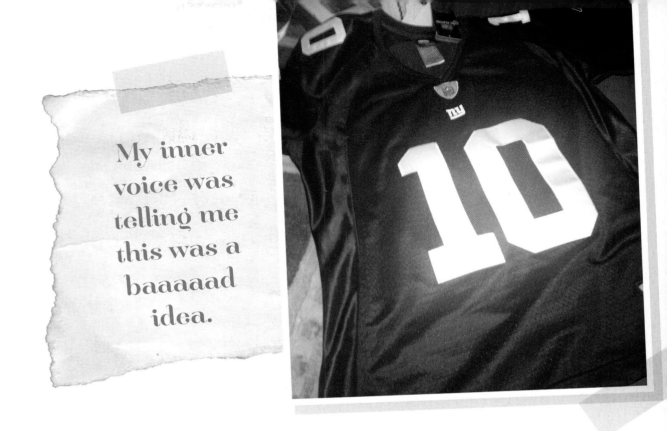

My inner voice was telling me this was a baaaaad idea.

year. Besides the fact that I'm a GIANTS fan, I was terrified of the idea. I've sung at Madison Square Garden before, but the football stadiums are much, much bigger. My inner voice was telling me this was a *baaaaad* idea.

I talked it out with my friend Jessica Szohr. I told her that I was scared to death.

"Why? You're going to be amazing!" she said. To her it sounded like a whole lotta fun. Big crowd, big muscly football players . . . what could be bad about that?

"Well, I've never sang the national anthem to that many people before," I explained.

"It's gonna be okay!"

"But anything can happen!" I insisted.

Honestly, what was the worst that could happen? I ticked off a few possibilities. I could get the hiccups. I could screw up the words. (Christina Aguilera already beat me to that.) My voice could crack. (No one was there for a concert—they were there to watch the game.) By talking it out, I realized that I was being ridiculous. What a great and awesome opportunity! And I shouldn't be afraid of what I do best. I visualized what it would be like (70,000 people! Eek!). I closed my eyes and saw myself singing in the middle of the field. It was so silent you could hear a pin drop. Then came the thunderous cheers and applause. Holding tight to that image, I took my time during the soundcheck and made sure I felt completely comfortable and confident. In the end, it was thrilling and a moment I will never forget. If I hadn't done it, I'd be kicking myself right now. Self-doubt will derail you in a heartbeat. And your own self-critic is tougher than any bully tossing slushies in your face.

> If I hadn't done it, I'd be kicking myself right now.

STUFF THAT SCARES THE CRAP OUT OF ME

- Bugs
- Spiders
- Snakes
- Heights (but I love roller coasters)
- Knives (but I love to cook)
- Needles
- Hospitals
- Hospital gowns (drafty!)
- Putting on a leotard with no advance warning
- Scary movies
- Imaginary people waiting in the back seat of my car when I get in it (thanks to watching too many scary movies!)
- Getting stuck in the bathroom with no toilet paper

93

talk yourself into it . . . not out of it

You can look at any situation and see both the good and the bad in it. Basically, you create your own reality. I talk myself out of a lot of negatives by saying it out loud to someone (like I did with my friend Jess). When I do, a weight is lifted. I just need to put it out there so it becomes tangible. I can get my arms around it and take control. There was one scene on *Glee* where I had to cry during the entire song because "I love Mike Chang so much" in the Valentine's Day episode. I didn't think I could do it with real emotion and also make it funny. Rehearsal time rolled around and my internal monologue went something like this: "What if I mess up? What if I'm not funny and the scene falls flat? Wait, what if I look stupid?" I forced myself to focus on all of the above and answer my own questions: "If you mess up, they'll shoot it again. You have ten more takes to get it right. If you're not funny, they'll cut the scene from the episode. And as for looking stupid . . . everyone here is your friend, and they're not going to think that!"

> **"What if I mess up? What if I'm not funny and the scene falls flat? Wait, what if I look stupid?"**

If you tell yourself you're going to fail, you will. It's that simple. You'll unconsciously sabotage every chance you have to succeed. There have been a few times in New York where I was on audition for a musical. I heard the music once or twice and decided I couldn't get through the song: it was too high or too belty or too *whatever*. I was so convinced I'd fail that I wouldn't practice or rehearse. I would avoid playing the music or even looking at it. I figured avoidance would make me feel less defeated. So in I would go, totally unprepared, and (you guessed it) blow the audition. Later on, I learned that I could tackle any song, no matter how tough, if I just ran through it and stayed positive.

Heartwork
Assignment
9

AM I a dRaMa QUEEN?

Be honest—how would you handle the following situations?

You landed a job interview with a huge record producer. It goes great, but on the way out, you accidentally trip. You:

A) *Laugh it off and send a thank-you e-mail for a great meeting.*

B) *Crawl out the door on your belly, mortified, and assume you're the last person on the planet he would hire.*

Your best friend calls to say she can't make it to the movies with you tonight—something came up. You:

A) Call up another pal and catch the midnight showing of Breaking Dawn—Part 2.

B) Spend the rest of the evening plotting your revenge— how dare she make you miss R-Patz?

The cashier overcharges you $2 for your bagel and coffee this a.m. You:

A) Shrug it off—everyone makes mistakes.

B) Assume this is a sign from the gods: the rest of the day is going to suck big time.

You break a nail on the way to work. You:

A) Pick up some Krazy Glue at the drugstore and do a quick repair job.

B) Sob hysterically—you just got a mani yesterday!

Your guy forgets today is your six-month anniversary. You:

A) Gently remind him by writing "Happy Anniversary" in toothpaste on the bathroom mirror.

B) Kick his butt to the curb. No man ever forgets you and lives to talk about it!

IF YOU ANSWERED MOSTLY A'S: You've got a well-balanced outlook on life. You keep it all in perspective.

IF YOU ANSWERED MOSTLY B'S: You deserve an Academy Award for your performances. (Move over, Meryl Streep!) But is throwing a hissy fit gonna get you anywhere? Instead, rethink how you react to situations. Is there a calmer, kinder, gentler approach you can take?

would you rather be right . . . or happy?

I am stubborn, and I don't like being wrong. Blame it on the fact that I'm a Taurus—we bulls like everything our way. On occasion, I'll disagree with my boyfriend Michael, and neither of us will want to give in. We go around in circles, arguing over something, until we're both pissed and frustrated. For what? Because I'm too stubborn to admit I was wrong? Life is too short. Every now and then you have to suck it up and say, "Sorry . . . I was wrong." We all make mistakes; we're human. There's a lot to be said for walking in someone else's shoes and

seeing things from their viewpoint. I admit, it's a tough lesson for me, but I'm working on it. When I accept that I am not perfect and not all-knowing, I open myself up to so many more possibilities. Being wrong is actually very liberating—and it does wonders for your relationship!

"Live in the moment and be present in all that you do. Don't worry yourself with what happened yesterday or what's going to happen tomorrow. Stay focused with what's in front of you."

—Michael Trevino (my man !)

outta my way!

So what, exactly, is holding you back from doing something that could be amazing/exciting/life-changing? Lack of knowledge? Experience? Connections? What can you do to change this? People kept telling me, "You have to take dance if you want to be on Broadway." I didn't want to take dance. I knew it wasn't my thing. But I also knew that one day a casting agent was going to ask me to shuffle across the stage, and I'd probably fall over my own two left feet. So I took ballet, tap, jazz, modern . . . they weren't easy, but they came in handy when I was a swing in *Spring Awakening*. Now on *Glee* people say, "Jenna can do it all." I may not be exceptionally great at one thing, but I can handle myself. I'm a multitasker!

I loved animals and thought maybe I'd become a veterinarian.

Sometimes we let ourselves get in the way of . . . well, ourselves. In the case of my Valentine's song on *Glee*, it was definitely fear of falling flat on my face. We are stronger than that. Some of us know exactly what we want to do and exactly how we are going to get there. I was always the girl putting on shows in my basement with costumes, so the stage was my first career choice. But toward middle school, even after having performed professionally, I suddenly wasn't sure I wanted to keep acting. I loved animals and thought maybe I'd become a veterinarian. Then after college, after earning my bachelor's in acting, I wasn't getting very many jobs. Once again, I pondered, "Do I ditch this idea and do something else? Maybe this isn't for me?" That's when I thought maybe I wanted to be a makeup artist or a personal trainer.

There have been many times in my life when I have been very confused. Have patience. Look for things that make you happy and smile every day. There is a passion and fire in each one of us, and you will figure it out. If you search hard enough, your calling will eventually find you. Until then, keep your eyes and your mind open—and be prepared to take a few leaps and fall on your butt.

Will it fall...will it stay? I love living on the edge!

100

Whenever I'm feeling negative I draw an "x" on my hand to remind myself to stay positive!

101

MiNd Games

Sometimes you're not even aware that you're being indecisive (am I?). Take this quiz and see if you make up your mind with conviction or waffle your way though life.

My greatest strength is:

A) I'm not sure . . . give me a sec.

B) I have lots of strengths; I can't choose just one.

C) My ability to make a decision and stick to it.

My greatest weakness is:

A) Ben & Jerry's . . . Domino's Pizza . . . Glee or . . . Ryan Gosling

B) That's tough—it's hard to pick just one!

C) My big heart.

Your best friend says, "Where should we go tonight?" You reply:

A) "How about a movie . . . or a club. Maybe bowling?"

B) "Whatever you want. I don't care."

C) "I want to see the new Hunger Games flick, STAT!"

Your boyfriend says he's starved. You:

A) Toss a ton of takeout menus on the table and spend a half hour looking through them for ideas.

B) Say, "Whatever you feel like, honey buns."

C) Phone in for Mexican—burritos it is, babe.

You interview for two jobs and land them both. You:

A) *Say yes to the first . . . and to the second. Now what will you do?*

B) *Stall—you need to weigh the pros and cons a couple of times first and ask your family's and friends' opinions.*

C) *Choose the one with the most opportunity for career growth and negotiate the salary.*

IF YOU ANSWERED MOSTLY A'S: You should probably enroll in Indecisives Anonymous. How do you even decide what to wear in the morning? Try to trust your instincts more and doubt yourself less.

IF YOU ANSWERED MOSTLY B'S: You're a moderate waffler—you like to think every decision over very, very carefully. You might try less looking and more leaping. Maybe you'd get further!

IF YOU ANSWERED MOSTLY C'S: You know your mind and aren't afraid to assert yourself. Just make sure your actions aren't impulsive. It's great to know what you want; just consider the consequences of getting it.

5 minutes to glee
SCARE YOURSELF SILLY

Need a mood-altering movie experience? Pop in *The Exorcist* and watch a scene. Fans of horror flicks will tell you there's a great adrenaline rush that comes from being literally scared out of your seat. That's because adrenaline also produces endorphins (those happy chemicals in your brain). Screaming at some slasher on the screen is also a great way to let out stress and anxiety. When the credits roll, your body returns to a calmer state. Bring it on, Freddy Krueger.

Me, Michael, and Claire Holt clowning around.

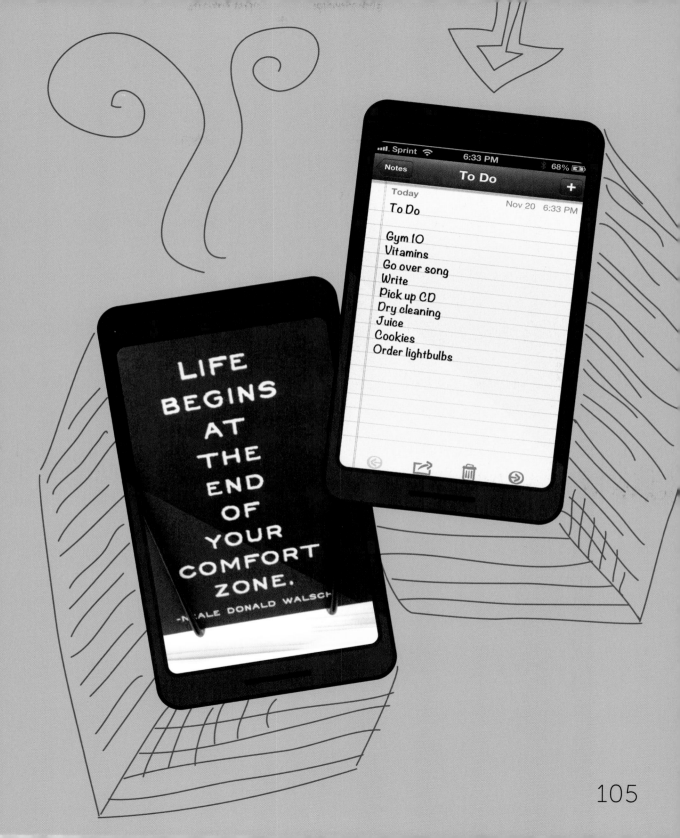

RULE 4
READY, SET...
SCREW UP

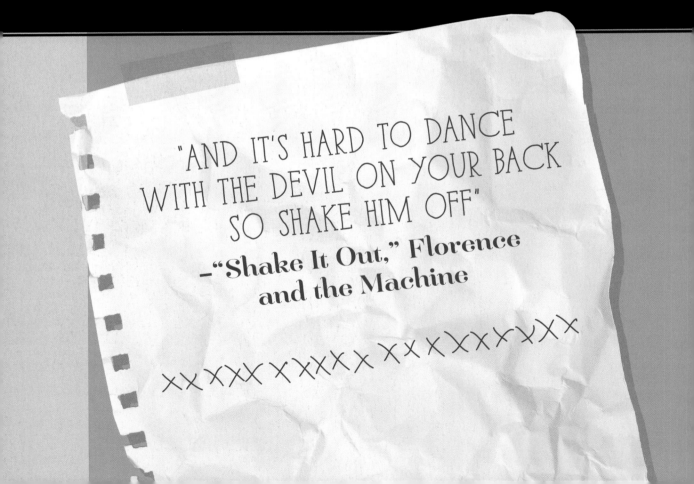

"AND IT'S HARD TO DANCE
WITH THE DEVIL ON YOUR BACK
SO SHAKE HIM OFF"
–"Shake It Out," Florence
and the Machine

107

no one, I repeat, NO ONE is perfect. You will make mistakes. I sure as hell did. I messed up horribly on the *Glee* audition; I completely skipped a whole verse. I did thirty-two bars from "Waiting for Life to Begin," and thought I blew it. I was at Ripley-Grier Studios in New York City. It was me, the accompanist, the casting director, Ryan Murphy, and some of our other executive producers. I was nervous, and on top of it, I had just made a new cut to the music—meaning I had chosen a few sections of the song I wanted to sing out of order. The music began, and I messed up the words, and then went off tempo. It snowballed from there: the accompanist and I were trying to catch up to each other, and I finished the song out of breath and aggravated. I tried to blame it on the guy, but he was having none of it. "Maybe you should try another cut," he smirked at me. Thanks, pal.

I left that room thinking there was no way in hell I was getting cast in *Glee*. Not when I showed them I was incapable of reading music, memorizing lyrics, or staying on key. But Ryan and everyone saw through it and obviously took a chance on me. I'll be forever grateful . . . and forever dumbfounded by my luck.

Another time, when I was fourteen, I went to a dance call and walked out in the middle of learning the dance combination. Instead of giving it a shot, I threw in the towel. I just said, "I hurt my ankle," and walked out the door. I picked up my bag and left; I didn't even try to do it. I was afraid of embarrassing myself in front of my peers. What a totally a stupid thing to do. I completely killed any chance I had. But I learned from it. I will never walk out again. There have been so many times on *Glee* episodes when the choreographer introduces a dance routine and I think, "Yeah, right!

How will I ever do that?" But I do it—at least I make a damn good effort. Even if I trip over my own feet (or someone else's!), I try. So was it worth screwing up when I was 14? You betcha. It made me a braver, more dedicated performer. I may never be as good as dancer as Heather or Harry, but I get an A for effort!

It's important to take responsibility for your actions—the good, the bad, and the ugly. Own them. If you're going to make a choice, go with it. Whether they're right or wrong, stand by your actions and focus on what you've learned. What has your mistake taught you about yourself and the world around you? What are the valuable life lessons you can take away from this experience and build upon? I try never to think of a mistake as failure—it's feedback! If I didn't study my lines the night before a big scene or you didn't study for that test, you didn't fail… you just didn't *try*. You made a mistake and that's okay, but don't do it again. In my case, I learned that nothing ventured equals nothing gained. I've now learned that I can't always limp out of an audition (like I did with my "bum ankle") if it looks tough. I have to buckle down and give it my best . . . and maybe take a few more dance classes so I don't blow the combination again!

A mistake is just a temporary pause in your plan. It's not the end; it's not a reason to throw in the towel, tempting as that may be. I hate to dwell on mistakes; I try to wash them from my memory. When you do screw up, cut yourself some slack. ALLOW yourself to make a mistake (or several), and don't beat yourself up over it. You can't let a mistake knock you down. It's just one moment, one day. There will be others. You can also go vent, write in your journal, go get an ice cream sundae and watch a rom-com. Relax, let yourself feel, then move on and get out of the funk.

FUHGEDDABOUDIT!
LETTING GO OF MISTAKES

It's 2 a.m., and you're wide awake, staring at the ceiling. A mistake you made is playing over and over again in your mind like a broken record. The more you think about it, the more anxious and inept you feel. Been there; done that. Want my advice? Let it *gooooo*! Here's how:

Allow yourself to feel bad. You screwed up; it sucks. You're entitled to feel disappointed, angry, guilty, or frustrated—even all of the above. But don't keep the pity party going forever. Don't wallow. Feel it, and then set those emotions free. I like to journal my feelings: "I am really pissed at how today's rehearsal went. I was off my mark." Once I've put them out there in the universe, I can move on.

What's done is done. Accept and acknowledge that past mistakes are now out of your hands. You can't hit "rewind" on your day or ask for a do-over. When you wrap your brain around this, the stress melts away.

Give yourself some credit. You did the best you could in the time/situation you were in.

Focus on what you can do now to avoid repeating this mistake. What will you do differently, and what lessons can you take away? What insights have you learned about yourself and the world in general?

Remember that everyone makes mistakes. It's called being human. If you're not failing, you're probably not doing enough to challenge yourself.

Mistakes make the man (or woman). Your mistakes don't define your future, but how you handle them does. Do you face them with style? Dignity? Grace? Guts? Or do you fall apart at the seams? This says a lot about your character. What kind of person do you want to be?

Keep your focus on the finish line. It's like running a marathon—just stay on course in the right direction till you get to your destination, even if it takes you hours and miles to get there. Think of that mistake as a hurdle you have to leap over. Once you do, it's behind you.

oops, i did it again!

If I tally them up (please, don't make me!), I have made tons of mistakes in my life. Here are a few repeat offenses that most people make—do these sound familiar?

MISTAKE #1 **I said something inappropriate/blurted something out and hurt someone's feelings.** My friend asked a group of friends if she should get a dog. I replied, "That poor dog," because she could barely take care of herself. I didn't mean to say it. It just came out. She got really upset; I embarrassed her in front of everyone. I apologized later and explained that I didn't think it was the right time in her life to get a dog. She didn't have a steady paying job and was in debt. I pointed out that if God forbid the dog got sick, vet bills weren't cheap. She saw my point, but I wish I had been kinder and gentler about making it! At least I said I was sorry and owned up to being insensitive.

LESSON LEARNED Do not open mouth/insert foot. Think before acting on an emotion. Recognize when you're worked up emotionally and remove yourself from that charged situation. If you do something wrong, uncaring, or uncalled for, then admit it was out of line. Don't pass the blame; don't shrug it off like it was no biggie. Just admit it and make it right again.

MISTAKE #2 **I spilled the beans.** I'm pretty much a vault when it comes to secrets, but when I was working at a restaurant, one of my friends told me in confidence she was dating one of the waiters. I was being chit-chatty, and I told another waitress the dirt I'd learned. Her face turned white. She said, "I've been seeing him, too!" It wasn't pretty, and I started a major war between them.

LESSON LEARNED Gossip is never good news. Somebody's business is not mine to share. Note to self: Keep mouth shut next time.

> Recognize when you're worked up emotionally and remove yourself from that charged situation.

MISTAKE #3 I keep thinking about a problem till I'm a
nervous wreck. Learning the "Gangnam Style" song for *Glee*
was one of the hardest things I've ever had to do, and I worked
myself up into a lather over it. I had to sing it in Korean, and I
kept procrastinating because I was so scared I would make a
huge fool of myself. How the heck do you pronounce, "Na je
nun ta sa ro un in gan jo gin yo ja?" It felt like I was speaking
in Furby. When I finally did it, it ended up being really fun, and
everyone was very impressed. Oppan Gangnam Style, baby!

LESSON LEARNED Don't overanalyze little things till they become big
and terrifying. Keep your perspective. Next time, I won't obsess and make
something a bigger problem than it is.

MISTAKE #4 I'm thinking of getting back with my ex . . .
A few short days after I broke up with my ex, I called him in a
moment of weakness and said I wanted to see him. He took me
to a concert, and we ran into some friends. He hit on my friend
right in front of me! I was reminded immediately why I broke up
with him in the first place: He was gross. People don't change,
especially that quickly!

LESSON LEARNED Going backward instead of forward is never a good
idea—especially since you broke up for a good reason. You may be lonely,
but history belongs in the past.

"I think the secret to happiness is being true
and honest to yourself while striving to be the
best person you can be. To love yourself and
others around you as if there is no tomorrow, to
be generous, compassionate, and forgiving. To
remember to enjoy the small, fleeting moments that
make the corners of your mouth reach for the skies."
—NINA DOBREV

MISTAKE #5 I put up with a person/situation I can't stand. I had a friend who would always flake on me. I always let him get away with it because he had great excuses, until he canceled on a vacation that I had planned. I was out the extra $ (his share) for the trip. That was the last straw. He didn't flake after that because I stopped inviting him to things that were important to me.

LESSON LEARNED Think about why you're friends with that person. Is it worth all the drama? Walk away from the drama and the people who create it before you get sucked into the abyss.

MISTAKE #6 I think I missed my chance. Once I was offered a role in a film a few years back. It was when we were touring for *Glee*. I had just come off the concert tour and a season of filming. I didn't want to pass up any acting opportunities, but it was my only time off before starting to shoot the next season. I had to say no because I needed some time off to sleep, go on a vacation, and rest up for the upcoming year. In retrospect, I'm glad I passed: I would have been exhausted, and I would have been letting down my show. Tina's role has become so much more complex, and I'm glad I made it my focus.

LESSON LEARNED You're exactly where you need to be. Don't think you've lost time. Every opportunity you've passed on has brought you to this moment, and every moment is a fresh chance to start again.

say what you mean and mean what you say

It sounds simple enough, but it's not always that easy to find your voice or summon the courage to use it. Case in point: I had to convince my parents to let me go to college in New York City when I was eighteen. I knew NYC was the place to be if you wanted to be an actress. Broadway was there, and I could easily go on auditions. But my folks were petrified. They couldn't stand the thought of their little girl in the big, bad city on her own. I cried at first; then I begged and pleaded, and when I realized that didn't work . . . Strike 2. I had to *show* them that I could learn how to do laundry on my own and manage the little money I had. I had to be independent but also listen to them when they asked me to do something. (This meant coming home at the hour they set.) When I was a little kid, I had a temper and used to throw tantrums. I even threw a mirror once, I was so angry. That didn't get me anywhere—except to my room with no TV. And this kind of behavior wasn't going to work for me now either, now that I was a "young adult." You have to take the higher road and communicate in a calm and mature manner. In the end, I talked to my folks calmly and maturely, and convinced them (through my neat

You have to take the higher road and communicate in a calm and mature manner.

and tidy room and respectful tone) to let me go to New York. I had to earn it. Earn their trust and my independence. That meant making mature decisions, and promising to check in with them. I told my mom and dad I would let them know I was safe and that I would work hard at school.

If you want to convince people to let you take risks and make your own mistakes, you can't throw a hissy fit. They don't mean to burst your bubble; they love and care about you, and they don't want to see you get hurt.

When it come to parents, I say pick your battles wisely. If you ask someone for something completely unreasonable ("Mom and Dad, can I have some money to buy a horse?") expect to be met with resistance. But if it's something you're really passionate about—in my case, a career in acting and the college of my choice—then fight for it. Do anything and everything you can to make them see things from your perspective.

fight fair:
how to win an argument

As an actor, sometimes you find a director sees it one way, and you see it another. It's bound to happen. Not everyone is coming from the same place and perspective. It's kind of like when you don't agree with a grade your teacher gave you on a test and you want to talk about it (maybe even get him/ her to rethink it!). Sometimes, I don't agree with the director's vision for a scene. In rehearsal before we shoot, we might talk about what we both want to get out of the scene and how we can best achieve this. On *Glee* I've never had any HUGE disagreements because everyone is so agreeable. We know we're all in it together and want the best for our show. But I will definitely stand up for myself and my character. If something doesn't feel right for Tina, I might say, "Tina would never do that." On one episode, the script called for Mr. Schue to pick a song for regionals and for the whole glee club to cheer. I thought about it, and then I piped up, "I think Tina would be upset that she didn't get the lead vocal. I don't think she would be happy at this moment." The director nodded and said, "You have a good point. Just try one happy and see how it reads." I did, and then we did another take the way I thought she would feel it—angry and disappointed. For the record, I won!

Arguing your point is tricky. You can hire yourself an attorney (pricey!), or just try the following:

Build your case. Don't head into World War III without ammunition. Do your homework; prove why you are making the best, well-informed decision.

Be logical. What is the one thing your opponent can't argue with? What would he/she understand the most?

Keep your cool. If you lose it, you'll lose. Stay calm; speak, don't yell. You'll be heard a lot better.

Don't resort to low blows like Sue slinging hair insults at Mr. Schue. Come on, you're better than that.

Listen up. Your opponent may have a good, solid point. Hear him/her out; what are the concerns and doubts? For example, your best friend hesitates when you suggest she go to a party with you. You can't understand why she wouldn't want to go. Maybe what you didn't know was that she just got turned down by a guy—who happens to be going to the party with another girl. Now it makes sense, right? But you would never know that unless you let her speak her mind.

Find a compromise, something that might work for both of you. Your boyfriend feels like lasagna, and you want sweet and sour chicken. Settle on something in between, like a Hawaiian pizza (sweet and saucy!). Or you pick the main course, and he gets to decide dessert. Fair and square!

5 minutes to glee
smell the roses

Literally! When you're having a bad day, go out and buy yourself a bouquet of flowers and breathe them in. The pretty blooms don't just brighten your room; they also release a special form of oxygen that's easy for your lungs to absorb. Experts say that's a quick and easy way to make you feel more relaxed in seconds. Note to boyfriend: Flowers and chocolate are the way to this happy girl's heart!

RULE 5
EXPECT THE UNEXPECTED

"I DON'T CURSE WHAT I CAN'T CHANGE, I JUST PLAY THE HAND I'M DEALT."
—Stephen Schwartz,
Children of Eden

Life is constantly in motion—like some crazy amusement park ride that takes your breath away. At any given moment, you can be hurled upside down at a dizzying pace. You always have a choice: Which way do you want to go? Will you cower . . . or find your courage?

Remember how I begged to go to New York? Well, I found out I didn't like college too much. I attended Marymount Manhattan College from 2004 to 2007, but I soon realized college was not for me. I felt like it was a distraction from what I really wanted to be doing: auditioning and performing. And I wasn't learning anything from sitting in a classroom. I wanted to be living and experiencing everything I could. Besides the requirements for my major like Theatre History, Musical Theatre, and Playwriting, I had to take Quantitative Reasoning and Science, which I felt were unnecessary for my goals as an actor. I felt so torn. For a while I was trying to do both: while

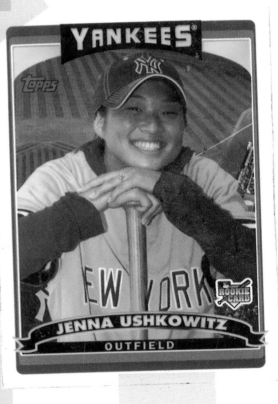

going to school I was also working full-time, traveling, and hosting a TV show for the Yankees—a half-hour show geared toward giving kids a behind-the-scenes look at baseball. I would go around to different places in the United States and "report" on how a baseball glove is made, how spring training was going, or just be a foul ball girl for the day. It was a paying professional job, something I could put on my resume, so I couldn't refuse.

Me and Jorge Posada—
an amazing catcher for the
New York Yankees

Me in Derek Jeter's
batting helmet

I did it for three seasons during college, so I missed a lot
of class. The college threatened to fail me—show up or get
out. They sent home a letter to my parents saying that I was
in danger of failing. (As you can imagine, that did not go over
very well!) I went to my advisor, and he explained to me that
performance classes aren't like lectures. They don't stand for
you just showing up a few times and getting the notes from
friends. You physically have to be there to perform and do the
exercises and necessary assignments.

After much debate, I decided to make it work. I promised
my teachers I'd show up for class more often, and I told
the Yankees people that they had to work around my class
schedule. It was hard making both sides happy, but I didn't go

123

to college to chuck it. I'm so glad today that I stayed in school, even though it would have been so much easier to drop out. But it was hearing the threat of "you're going to fail" that snapped me back. I do not handle failure well. It pisses me off. Not acceptable. Instead, I decided to graduate in three years instead of four. It meant taking on a lot more classes all at once (even during my vacation breaks) and squishing in more courses, but if it got me out the door sooner, it was worth it.

"The secret to happiness is knowing that perfection is a fantasy and having flaws just makes you unique and special. If you can find a way to love and accept yourself flaws and all, you will find happiness."

—Amber Riley

when life throws you a curveball . . .

Be flexible, open-minded, willing to chuck your plan and come up with a better one if it will help you get closer to your goal. My friend Adrien Finkel was one of the first people I hung out with when I moved to LA. At the time, she was pursuing an acting career. But after four years, it just wasn't happening for her. She didn't flip out because things didn't work out. Instead, she discovered a love for cooking and baking. She took a cooking class and got a job as a chef at a great management company. Around the same time, she was also taking photographs and learning to use a camera. She was loving the photography and came up with http://www.wordswithfriendsproject.com because words have always affected and inspired her. So she decided to ask her friends what words inspire them, and now she travels the country shooting pics and collecting words of wisdom. I am so proud of her! She's a prime example of being open to new possibilities and finding a path that makes you truly happy.

→ **Think out of the box.** How can you do something different with the situation that's been presented to you? Nothing is crazy; nothing is impossible. A few years ago, people told Ryan that a musical on TV every week was a crazy idea. Who would want to watch a bunch of neurotic kids sing and dance? Aren't you glad he didn't listen?

→ **Keep laughing.** Have a sense of humor when the shit hits the fan. Luckily, I have some pretty funny co-stars on *Glee*. They don't let me stress out; Chord likes to pull pranks and do impressions, and Amber always keeps us laughing. She'll give people wet willies, take Kevin's glasses so he can't see, or snap silly pictures and post them.

→ **Everything happens for a reason.** I fully believe in synchronicity. Mr. Hoare always told me that synchronicity is a sign that you're on the right path and in the right place at the right time. Nothing is really coincidence. Sometimes opportunities come and go in the blink of an eye, and if they don't work out, it's because something else is going to happen. Trust the universe. Case in point: If *Spring Awakening* had never happened, *Glee* might have been just a passing thought. The New York casting associate for *Spring Awakening* was holding the auditions for *Glee*. A few months later, I got a call from my agent that I was going to be reading for Ryan Murphy, Brad Falchuk, and Dante Di Loreto. I was hired a month later as Tina.

Trust your gut and your instincts. They always take you in the right direction. As long as you are working hard and toward a goal, the signs along the way will indicate the right path. When I auditioned for *Glee*, Ryan asked me who I thought Tina was. I had nothing to draw from except the pilot script, so I just had to go with my gut. I said I felt just like Tina at times. I was the one who used theater, music, etcetera as an outlet. I also thought that being in a glee club would be a great, positive step in the right direction for her. Ryan smiled. "I'm glad you see her as so positive." It was the right answer because it was an honest answer. As an actor, improv is all about following your gut— you let the scene take you where it will.

As long as you are working hard and toward a goal, the signs along the way will indicate the right path.

learning from loss

In my sophomore year of high school, Joey, a boy I had known since second grade, took his own life. It was a huge shock to me; I couldn't fathom someone so young not wanting to live anymore. It seemed like such a waste, and my heart just ached for him and his family. Couldn't someone have helped him? Wasn't there any other way to find peace? I wrote poems and grappled with the fact that he wasn't coming back and that there was nothing I could do about it.

That same year, my family went through a very frightening medical emergency as well. My mom had to have open-heart surgery. She was in the hospital for two weeks and was very ill. I was terrified that something would go wrong and she wouldn't make it. All I wanted to do was sit by the side of her hospital bed. It was like everything else in my life suddenly receded into the background. My friends were all going to a party, but I had no interest. It all felt so trivial, so meaningless. Luckily, she came through the operation and

recovered fully. But the experience left me feeling strangely off-balance—as if I were walking a tightrope with no net. Was life truly this unpredictable? Was there anything I could count on *not* to change? Then a week after my high school graduation, I lost another friend in a drunk-driving accident. Christina was my predecessor as class president. Again, I struggled to wrap my mind around the idea that you can be here one day and gone the next. My parents tried to explain to me that life is a precious gift and that this was an important lesson to be learned from losing someone. I couldn't see it. Was I supposed to make lemonade out of lemons? Was I supposed to find something positive in this tragedy?

But as time went on and I grew up, I realized my parents are right. Whether you are fifteen or fifty, losing someone or something close to you shakes you to the core. It makes you question everything you value—What is meaningful? What is true?—and this is a good thing. Because if life is truly so fragile and fleeting, what are you doing wasting your time sweating the small stuff? Loss taught me a great deal about living:

Say "I love you." Tell your loved ones that you love them while they're here. Hug them and share what's in your heart—don't assume they know, and don't be embarrassed to be affectionate. Love is the strongest, most powerful force we possess as human beings.

Listen up. How many times have you asked someone, "Hey, how's it going?" but never even stopped to listen to the answer? Care—it's a very simple concept. Care about what makes people tick, and take time to hear them out.

Laugh often. Sorrow reminds us how lucky we are to have joy. Don't take yourself so seriously. Have fun; act silly; be footloose and fancy-free.

Live authentically. By this, I mean remind yourself who you are, and don't try to be someone you're not. If you only have a certain amount of time on this Earth to make an impact, then let the real you shine through.

Have faith. In yourself, in others, in the universe. Faith is what allows us to function in times of unpredictability. When I was worried about my mom's surgery, I prayed to a higher force. I'm not a very religious person, but it gave me hope and strength. Whether you believe in God or not, there is something truly comforting about acknowledging that some things are completely out of your hands and your control.

> There is something truly comforting about acknowledging that some things are completely out of your hands and your control.

WRITE A THANK-YOU NOTE

Expressing gratitude is a great way to shake a woe-is-me moment. Personally, I am an e-mail person: I like to drop a little instant "gracias" over the Internet if someone has done something nice for me: "Hey, Carrie! Thanks so much for sending me those yummy cupcakes!" You may prefer to pen a pretty notecard and send it snail mail. Whatever works. But make it a habit. Send out happy thoughts and you'll get them back in return.

Dear Mom,

I just want to say thank you for shaping me into the independent, strong woman I am today. Thank you for everything you've taught me: to believe in myself and never give up; to keep a good head on my shoulders with my feet on the ground; to treat everyone equally and never judge. When you insisted I invite everyone to my birthday party (not just the "cool" kids), I realize now that you were showing me one of the most important lessons in life. I will always carry it with me. You explained to me that no matter who you are, what you look like, or what you know, everyone is equally important and significant. You made me realize that everyone is beautiful, inside and out. You taught me to always take care of myself, work hard, and be the best I can be at all times. Because of you, I strive to be an honest, open, and loving person. You care for everyone else and always put them first. It will always be your flaw, but I have taken it and made it my flaw as well.

You encouraged me to take risks and make mistakes because you will always be there to catch me when I fall. I have always been the happy, gleeful baby that smiled in your arms for the first time. Because of you, I am who I am. So thank you. I love you.

RULE 6
Get OFF YOUR BUTT

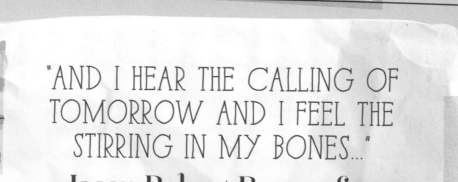

"AND I HEAR THE CALLING OF
TOMORROW AND I FEEL THE
STIRRING IN MY BONES..."
–Jason Robert Brown, from
Songs for a New World

the best way to get "unstuck" in your life is to break the chains keeping you there. Are you on autopilot? Are you in a place you don't want to be but don't know how to leave? Time to take the wheel and drive.

When I was twenty and living in New York, I got a job as a hostess at a restaurant called Quality Meats on West 58th Street. It was a brand-new restaurant at the time, and my friend Arlae told me that they needed hostesses. They were paying $12.00 an hour, which was more than I was getting to work at Equinox gym. Count me in!

I found out pretty quickly it wasn't as good as it sounded. I had to wear a dress and high heels and go up and down two flights of stairs about one hundred times a night carrying drunkies' martinis and wine to their tables—all without spilling or tripping! We'd get yelled at by the maître d' if we sat the wrong table or got an order wrong; and customers generally treated us like crap if their table wasn't available immediately. One time a woman was so rude that I hid in the coat check to cry. I promised myself that day that I'd never let anyone make me cry or feel that small or unimportant again. I knew I was a lot smarter than this, and for what? A measly paycheck that barely paid the rent wasn't worth it for me. I wanted to do something, anything, else. So I asked the guy I was dating at the time to teach me to bartend. I had to learn everything from how to mix a dirty martini to what wines go with what food. It was a lot of work. Some people like to measure, but I learned by eyeballing (which is just guesstimating how much liquor you're pouring in— usually a recipe for a hangover). I got a few drinks sent back when I started, broke a lot of glasses, and got a lot of cuts on my hands. It was a lot of fun once I got the hang of it, but it took tremendous focus. The good news was I made money off of tips, and on a good night, I could walk away with anywhere between $400–$500 cash.

So the moral of this story? If you don't like the place you're in, find a way to move. I always believe that if you're not happy, you have to change things, or you'll eventually go mad as a hatter!

"After graduation, I had all these set ideas of which direction I wanted to take my life. I'm actually doing quite the opposite and I've never been happier. So, I guess the secret to happiness is not being afraid to let life surprise you. I never thought I'd be where I am today, but I couldn't have written it better. Work hard, enjoy the ride."
—DANTE RUSSO (MY FRIEND AND PARTNER IN CRIME)

take action

Stop waiting for someone else (your mom, your dad, your sibling, your friend) to do it for you. No excuses. No passing the buck. Get off your ass, and bring about the change you want to see. Don't wait for something to happen; make it happen. Like Tina says on *Glee*, in the "Born This Way" episode, "Be the change you want to see in the world." You can dream it; you can plan it, but until you take that first step, it's not gonna happen.

your ideas are never too big

For anyone who thinks his or her dream is impossible, remember that your vision can never be too big. Chris Colfer is a perfect example. He says that kids bullied him in school and called him terrible, abusive names in the hallways. He came from a small town, but he always knew he was destined for greatness. He always believed in himself and his genius. Now, at twenty-one, he's won a Golden Globe, written a book, written a screenplay, and become an icon for the gay community. It wasn't an easy road for him, but he has made it an easier road for so many kids. His courage stems from how strong he had to be in high school.

What I think is coolest about Chris is watching him grow from this little nineteen-year-old kid with all these amazing ideas into such an accomplished and confident man. But I could've told you that was coming four years ago. We all knew those kids who ridiculed him would work for him one day. He's showing young people all over that anything is possible.

December 11, 2008 Times Square NYC

Words of Wisdom:
CHRIS COLFER

Chris is someone who is wise beyond his years. He inspires me and brings so much laughter to my life. I wanted to share that with you. So I asked, and he answered:

What was your high school experience like? Did you always feel different?

It was very difficult but prepared me for the future. I was very overachieving in my own way, but was never respected for it. I think it's good to have struggles, though; they round you out as a person. I've always felt like a "social llama," wandering the farm looking for a stable to put myself in. But stables in the rural world are the equivalent to labels in the real world, and I've never liked being categorized. It's cheesy when people say this, but my differences really did turn out being my greatest advantages.

> I'VE BEEN PUSHED DOWN MANY FLIGHTS OF STAIRS IN MY TIME, BUT I ALWAYS MANAGE TO FIND AN ELEVATOR.
>
> —CHRIS COLFER

How did you learn to march to your own beat?

I'm not sure I ever learned how to march but I definitely learned how to *adjust to my waddle*. I spent a lot of time trying to be other people but discovered it was much easier to just be myself.

Did you ever compare yourself to others?

Constantly! I still do that. I'd say some self-comparison is healthy, to keep yourself striving to be the best you can be, but you don't want to put outrageous expectations on yourself. For example, until I have Bill Gates's brains, Taylor Lautner's body, and Ellen DeGeneres's personality, I'm not sure I'll ever be fully content.

What people did you surround yourself with?

Ever since I was little I always had older friends. I grew up doing community theater and had amazing friendships with other actors in the shows I did. As soon as I got into high school I made BFFs with teachers and the lunch ladies. I was always more stimulated by people who had lived and learned and established themselves than peers who were trying to figure themselves out.

What makes you YOU?

The fact that I've never been able to take "no" for an answer. I've been pushed down many flights of stairs in my time, but I always manage to find an elevator.

What's the key to being your own person?

Accepting who you are and rolling with it, I'd say. Never forget what you bring to the table—and if you're going to a potluck never forget to bring *something* to the table. Responsibility is a BIG factor of being your own person.

What makes you happy?

Planning.

it's not the last supper

By this I mean don't get trapped into thinking the change you make in your life at this moment is going to be forever. I promise you can change your mind later. Your passions and pursuits should continue to evolve. Maybe your goal this month is to get a job waiting tables. Great. It pays the rent. But maybe your long-term goal is to be an actress on Broadway, or a doctor, or a congressperson. Baby steps are okay—not everyone knows what they want to be when they grow up or even what they want to be doing ten years from now. Allow yourself the freedom to try new things and get inspired.

> "The key to happiness is in this very moment, and knowing that life is just a series of moments"
>
> —MATT MAISTO, MY BEST FRIEND FOREVER

stop bitching

Complaining, moaning, and groaning about your current situation is not going to make things better. I know, I know: "It's not fair . . . some people get all the luck." What does that accomplish? Personally, that kind of negative thinking only makes me feel worse. Unless you were born in Buckingham Palace, there is no quick way to become rich, famous, or successful. It takes work. It takes being in the right place at the right time. It takes diligence and drive. It takes long hard hours and paying dues. Anyone who tells you it's easy . . . they're lying.

"EVERYBODY SAYS DON'T WALK ON THE GRASS / WELL, I SAY DO. . . ."
—*Anyone Can Whistle*

5 minutes to glee
CLEAN UP YOUR ACT

Whenever I am feeling slightly stressed or out of sorts, I make like Snow White and whistle while I work to tidy up my space. Clutter is burdensome; it weighs you down. When you put things in their place, not only can you find where you dropped your keys, but you also feel like a weight has been lifted. You don't have to wash windows or scrub toilets; just sort through the stuff in your junk drawer or organize the pile of papers on your desk. Cleanliness is next to happiness!

before

after

And still not clean enough for my OCD!

5 RULES YOUR MOM TOLD YOU THAT ARE WORTH BREAKING

(OR AT LEAST BENDING!)

1. "IF THE SHOE FITS, WEAR IT." The shoe may fit, but it may not be the right style shoe for you. Don't settle for less than you know you are worth.

2. "KEEP QUIET." Go on and make some noise! State your opinion. Don't be silent if something is worth speaking out about.

3. "WASH YOUR HANDS." Sometimes, it's worth getting your hands dirty! Roll up your sleeves and get down to business if there's something you truly, deeply want.

4. "EARLY TO BED, EARLY TO RISE." Makes for a pretty dull life. Allow yourself plenty of time to catch some z's, but don't miss a great party or chance to meet new people just because it's past your bedtime.

5. "NEVER QUIT A JOB UNTIL YOU HAVE ANOTHER ONE LINED UP." Well, I blew this one out of the water! As long as you can deal with losing the paycheck (in my case, it was so small, I never missed it), it's fine to get yourself out of that dead-end position and focus on the future. You'll save your sanity.

dump your slump

Anytime I've been in a career or personal slump, it's usually because I compromised my goals. I've wandered off the path, and my energy and motivation is sapped as a result. Luckily, it's not hard to get back on track.

Try this for starters:

Focus on one goal. Make it a small one that you can achieve easily and in little amount of time. My goal is:

List THREE THINGS that excite you about this goal:

1.

2.

3.

List the things that might be holding you back from achieving this goal. Is it money? Time? Fear? Embarrassment?

Commit to it. I will make my goal happen by:

145

never

RULE 7
never say never

"GONNA GIVE
EVERYTHING I HAVE,
IT'S MY DESTINY..."
—Justin Bieber,
"Never Say Never"

Okay, maybe I'm channeling the Bieb a bit here, but I do believe this: You can't ever see a challenge as something insurmountable. There is always a way if you want to find it. When people tell me something's impossible, it's like an open invitation for me to prove them wrong. Tell me I can't write an entire book in a few months while working like a dog on *Glee* and trying to have a personal life as well . . . we all know how that turned out, don't we? Whatever it takes to make things work, I will do it. Right now, I'm sitting in the hair chair at 6:30 a.m., sipping tea and working on this chapter while getting my hair blown out for this morning's shoot. I am the queen of multitasking, man!

Sometimes your happiness depends on you standing up for yourself. As I've said before, I hate confrontation—so this is a particularly tough rule for me to follow. But Tina and I are learning to do this more and more; we're becoming better at fighting for what we want and deserve.

At the end of Season 3, when Rachel passed the torch to Tina, it sparked a fire in her that gave her the confidence to push for more songs, lead vocals, and bigger roles in everything the glee club does. Tina Chang has moved out of the shadows, and I'm proud of her! Does she occasionally get sideswiped . . . you betcha. Santana steals the role of Rizzo right out from under her, but at least she's showing she's a force to be reckoned with. They'll think twice next time before passing her over!

I find that most appreciate it when I volunteer or ask to take on more responsibility.

I'm also making sure I speak up and let the *Glee* writers know I want to do more. Don't be afraid that people will think you're bossy or bitchy or too big for you britches. I find that most appreciate it when I volunteer or ask to take on more responsibility. It shows I'm committed.

HOW TO FIGHT FAIR

Unless you like living life as a doormat, confrontation is inevitable. It's probably my least favorite thing in the world because I like people to always see me as "The Nice One." I hate being criticized, so I don't like to criticize others. Luckily, I have learned over the years that there truly is an art to arguing your case.

Honor the Three No-Nos. No name-calling. No bringing up past disagreements. No involving others in the argument ("Hey, Kevin . . . what do you think about this?"). These are my three golden rules. None of the above will EVER help the situation.

Keep your cool. No matter how upset or pissed off you are, you don't want to lose control. There were many times when I wanted to hurl something at my ex's head, but I didn't. Breaking china feels good in the moment, but it's a mess to clean up and pricey to replace.

Think before you blurt it out. When you say something cruel and hurtful in anger, you put it out there . . . and you can't take it back. Yeah, you might feel like calling your brother a loser, but think about how that will make him feel and the damage it might do to your relationship. I always take a deep breath before speaking: It allows my brain at least a few seconds to process what is about to come out of my mouth.

Put yourself in someone else's shoes. There are two sides to every story, and if you want to be fair, you need to hear your opponent out. Where is he/she coming from? What is causing this conflict? Sometimes, just hearing someone's explanation—"I didn't blow you off. I was home with a stomach flu!"—makes perfect sense and solves things instantly.

Compromise. Go for the win-win. Is there something you both can agree on that would put this entire issue to bed?

149

don't give up if
it's important to you

Only you can decide what matters to you and what is worth
pursuing. Sometimes it's a passion; other times it's a yellow
dress. Let me explain: For my very first Golden Globe award
show (how exciting!), I had a definite opinion about what dress
I wanted to wear, and I wasn't going to let anyone talk me out
of it. Just so you understand, finding the perfect gown for the
Globes is a lot like shopping for your prom dress. Only a lot
more people are going to see you in it (like the whole entire
world!), so it's a bit more pressure. I knew it had to be canary
yellow. (Kinda reminds me of Big Bird and my *Sesame Street*
days!) I didn't have a stylist to help me find it, but that didn't
stop me from searching. I went to about six showrooms (a place
where designers lend their dresses to celebrities
to wear to events) and tried on about seventy
gowns before I found the one I wanted. People
tried to convince me to go with another color,
but I was adamant that this is what I wanted
to wear that night. It was such a sunny, happy
color (so *Glee* appropriate, since it was our first
Globe nomination!) and I wasn't going to be
swayed. To this day, people tell me it's the most
memorable dress I've ever worn. So I'm glad I stuck
to my guns!

> I knew my
> dress had
> to be
> canary
> yellow.

WHERE THERE'S A WILL (SCHUESTER), THERE'S A WAY!

Mr. Schue and the New Directions never take no for an answer. There is no greater example I can think of faith and persistence. Through slushies, Sue sabotage, and endless competitors who don't play fair, they never falter. *Glee* has taught me how to push through no matter what. From the grueling schedules to the times where I am having a bad day, I refuse to give up or give in—like when I was really homesick and sad one day on tour in Detroit and had to go out and perform a one-and-a-half-hour show. The *Glee* cast has shown me the meaning of the words strength and dedication. They were there for me, holding my hand and making me laugh and assuring me that everyone felt homesick at least once. In these past four years, I have learned that if I want something bad enough and work hard enough at it, I'll get it. And if I don't, I'll make another opportunity for myself that's even better than the last. I have learned to stand up for myself and my convictions. I've learned that life is not just about surviving, it's about thriving. Becoming an adult is realizing that you don't have all the same beliefs as your family and friends, and that's okay. You have that right. I used to be so scared to be "wrong." Now I own my thoughts and opinions, and I look for meaning in every song, every script, and every person I work with. To just "be" is not enough for me. I need to be like Will, always looking for a whole that's greater than the sum of all its parts.

Us at our *Glee* signing at Comic Con! My friend Stephanie took this from the balcony above.

153

spell out your self-confidence

Whenever I am feeling a momentary twinge of doubt, I get out a pen and some paper. I start with a name or a word, using each of the letters to inspire me to write a reason why I should remain on track. I have fun with it, letting the sentences flow freely. Choose whatever word you like: your name, your favorite sports team, an adjective that describes your goal. It goes like this:

H: **Hands to hold.** *I have lots of people who believe in me, and I can't let them down.*

A: **Awesome.** *The way I feel when I accomplish something and see it through from start to finish.*

P: **Perseverance.** *What separates the winners from the losers. I learned to spell this word in fifth grade, so it must have been for a damn good reason.*

P: **Pac-Man.** *That little yellow guy had ghosts crawling up his butt, but he didn't give up, did he?*

Y: *Y should I not give up? Because I've come this far. Because I can see my dream just around the bend. Because Y is also for "Yay!" and "Yippie!" and "Yahoo!" and those are all words you exclaim when you do something great (which I will).*

5 minutes to glee
READ A GREAT BOOK

It doesn't matter what you read—Harry Potter or *War and Peace*—as long as you find it uplifting and relevant to you. Reading is a great way to explore areas outside your comfort zone. It lets you consider different ideas and opinions and challenge your beliefs. I like to read young adult books like John Green's *The Fault in Our Stars* and *Looking for Alaska*. Yes, I'm guilty of reading the *Fifty Shades* trilogy in a week (for guilty fun!), but I also love Lauren Oliver's novel *Delirium* and other books that make me feel as well as think. I like to read on my Kindle at work in my trailer or at home on a quiet night. Lea and I are always with our Kindles; Kevin, Heather, Matt, Becca, and Melissa are more traditional with a book in hand on set. I like to see what everyone is reading and we swap suggestions—kind of like an unspoken book club.

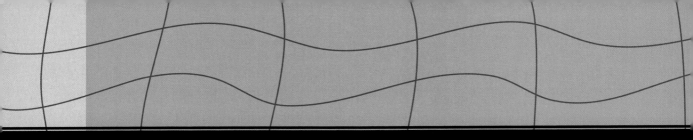

RULE 8
DO YOUR VERY BEST

"I'VE LIVED TO BE
THE VERY BEST. I
WANT IT ALL, NO
TIME FOR LESS"
–Whitney
Houston,
"One Moment
in Time"

159

i remember the day I was graduating college. I had come back late the night before from a gig with the Yankees in Ohio, so I was running on fumes. As I was unpacking and getting ready to flop into bed, I got a phone call from my agent.

"There's an audition tomorrow for a movie that you really should go for," she said.

I sighed. "Okay. What do I have to do for it?"

There was silence, then she spilled it: "Memorize twelve pages of dialogue."

Seriously? The last thing I wanted to do was study a script! But I stayed up all night, working on the script and getting it down. I didn't sleep a wink. Then, I went to the graduation ceremony at the church where I was singing a solo. After pictures, I changed out of my cap and gown and raced to the audition for the movie. (For the record, it went okay—but I didn't get the role.)

Then it was back to Lincoln Center where the second part of the ceremony was taking place. I realized I hadn't eaten since the night before, so I grabbed a cheeseburger and gulped it down just before the first strains of "Pomp and Circumstance"

> But I stayed up all night, working on the script and getting it down. I didn't sleep a wink.

began to play. After the ceremony part two, I went to dinner and then out to celebrate my degree with friends. I give myself a pat on the back for getting through that crazy day—and for giving it my all. I could have bagged the audition; I could have shown up late to graduation and caught a few z's. But both were important to me, so I tried my best. Which brings me to a very important piece of advice: Try. Try your hardest. That is all anyone can ever ask of you and all you can ever ask of yourself. Whatever the outcome, you gave it your all, and that alone deserves applause.

Try. Try your hardest.

push your limits

I'll let you in on a little secret: I did not think I had a great singing voice for a very long time, and I still have insecurities about it. I could always carry a tune, and I knew that my voice sort of sounded very similar to the kids I'd hear on Broadway, but I know I'm not the best. I have definitely worked very hard to train and get a voice that I feel strong and proud of, but I'll NEVER be as good as the Idina Menzels or the Kristin Chenoweths of the world. That's just a fact. But I don't let that stop me from being the very best I can be.

I had an amazing voice teacher, John Farrell, in high school who was convinced there was a voice inside of me that I didn't even know I had. He put me on daily practice schedules: warm up, breathe, sing, emote. I practiced endlessly in the shower, on my way to school, before bed. I always had my tapes available to listen to and my charts to keep track of my hours. I took his advice, and at auditions for the school musical the next year, out came this huge, powerful belt. I think I was just as shocked as everyone else to hear it! It taught me that if I work hard, I can get to where I want to be.

Another great teacher and motivator was the amazing director Paris Barclay, who has produced and directed many hit TV shows, including *NYPD Blue, ER,* and *Sons of Anarchy*. He probably has a closet filled with Emmys, so needless to say I was humbled to be in his presence. In Season 1, he came to direct an episode of *Glee* called "Wheels." In it, there was an intensely emotional scene where Tina admits to Artie that she's been faking her stutter. Barclay wanted me to do something on screen I'd never done before—cry. When I told him I wasn't sure I could do it, he shared a story. He told me about how Mike Nichols wanted Elizabeth Taylor to cry in *Who's Afraid of Virginia Woolf?* so he slapped her. I think between the adrenaline, his story, and being so scared (both of screwing up and getting slapped!), I just put myself in Tina's shoes. I imagined how upset she would be; she had just lost Artie as a boyfriend and a friend. The tears came streaming. It didn't feel good to cry, but it felt great to get where I needed to for the scene, to push myself and open myself up.

get out of your head

I used to get embarrassed having to kiss someone who wasn't my boyfriend. On *Glee*, I had to kiss Kevin . . . then Harry. I was so not comfortable. It kind of felt like a weird out-of-body experience; I was analyzing every second of it, watching myself go through the motion. Eric Stoltz, one of our directors, used to make us kiss in every episode just to be funny. He thought it was a riot that Mike and Tina make out and then that it never makes it into the cuts of the episode. I'm used to it now, but in the beginning, I was paranoid about *how* I kissed. Did I smudge my lipstick? Did I look like a fish? Then it became like a desensitization exercise: The more I smooched, the less it bugged me. Eventually, I just learned to go with the flow and trust my co-stars. Harry and I began to have fun with it. We'd eat something gross like a bag of salt and vinegar chips right before we had to lip-lock, just to gross each other out! It lightened the mood and always made us laugh! And frankly, when your partner's breath stinks, that's all you can think about; not the way your lips lock on camera.

Harry and I on set. What's wrong Harry?!

"Balance is the key. It's all pretty simple. When you lose balance on a tight rope, you fall. When you gain balance, it takes the effort of your whole body and adjustment to your core to get across successfully. It takes balance in your business, personal and love life to get closer to that thing we call happiness."

—HARRY SHUM

expect nothing less from yourself than your best

If you go into a task thinking, "I'm gonna suck at this," guess what? You will. I can almost guarantee it. It's the power of suggestion. Negative expectations and negative thoughts can only breed negative results. If you want to expect the best out of life, you first need to expect the best out of yourself. Be like that little engine that said, "I think I can." It will propel you to do much more than you think you're capable of. There have been times when I had to really push myself to do my best on *Glee*. When Tina had to be a "bitch" in the first few episodes, I wasn't sure that I could pull it off without being campy or fake. Kevin McHale, who always has my back, reassured me that I could be a bitch if I really tried hard. (Thanks, Kev!) So I decided to agree with him—I would do this and do it well. I would give it 110

The girls during "Summer Nights." We shot at the same high school as the original movie!

percent. I would crank up the attitude. In the end, it was a lot of fun, and I was proud for stretching myself and my character. I was proud that instead of whining "I can't do this," I told myself "You *will* do this."

> I WAS PROUD THAT INSTEAD OF WHINING "I CAN'T DO THIS," I TOLD MYSELF "YOU WILL DO THIS."

practice makes perfect

This goes for anything and everything in life. Sure, some people are natural God-given talents. (Kristin Chenoweth opens her mouth and the voice of a 6-foot-4 woman comes out of her 4-foot-8 body!) The rest of us need to work, work, work to get good at something. When I was younger (and okay, even now), my rhythm wasn't the best. I've always had to break down a dance and slowly find the beat. In fifth grade, my best friend Dana and I were the lead tappers in the dance club number "Putting on the Ritz." Everything we did had to be syncopated and in unison. We had to practice in her basement every day (so we wouldn't mess up her parents' wood floors upstairs), with her going over each step for hours and hours till it sunk in to my thick head.

A sociologist recently declared that it takes 10,000 hours of honing your skills if you want to be a success at anything. I don't know if we spent that long in Dana's basement, but I do agree with the basic principle. The more you train your brain/ your body to do something, the more it becomes a reflex—like second nature. I practice my lines for *Glee* right up until the moment the director shouts "Action!" Dana would be proud.

KRISTIN, THE CUPCAKE

The first time I got to work with Kristin Chenoweth (one of my theater idols) was in the first season of *Glee* in the "Preggers" episode. She's since become my all-time favorite guest star on *Glee*. I remember Chris Colfer and I were beside ourselves with excitement and nervous energy. We couldn't wait for her to arrive on set, and we came up with a code word so we could prepare ourselves when she walked into the rehearsal room. We kept watch out the window. "Okay," Chris whispered to me. "Whoever sees her coming first, say 'Cupcake!'" Little did we know how appropriate that word was for Kristin. She's this itty-bitty adorable thing, just bursting with sweetness and positivity. It was literally like a ray of sunshine entered the room. She's also a musical genius. It took the Glee Club three hours to learn the song "Last Name." Kristin nailed it in about forty-five minutes. The woman may be a cupcake, but she knows her stuff!

keep your promises

. . . to yourself and to others. Don't give up if something is hard or new or different. It took me a long time to get a great collaborator to help me get this book on its feet. I met with a lot of people and creatively we just didn't click. It took a year, and I was really frustrated and tempted to give up. I just wanted to throw

167

everything away and quit. But this is my passion project, and I made a promise to myself that I would make it happen. I didn't give up. I kept talking to people, explaining my vision, and I kept writing. Now here it is! If you say you'll do it, then do it. Follow through. When you break a promise, even a small one, it says to the person you are disappointing, "I don't value or care about you." It shows that you are someone who can't be counted on.

Break enough promises and you'll destroy a relationship. I am always very understanding when friends flake out on plans because they worked all day or something else came up but do it more than a few times and there better be a damn good reason why you can't make it. Breaking a promise to yourself is the same as disrespecting yourself. It's bad news for your self-esteem and confidence. Sometimes, I would waltz into dance rehearsal at *Glee* somewhere between one and ten minutes late and not think twice about it—until I started showing up on time and wondering where everyone else was. Our choreographer made a great point by illustrating "my time is just as valuable as yours." I never broke that time "promise" again.

There is no law that says you have to make promises—it's okay to say no. I've realized that it's very easy to trap myself into committing to too much. I said yes to be in

At an event with Dante DiLoreto (our executive producer) and our choreographer Zach Woodlee!

168

my best friend Tara's wedding party last year. Luckily, she's awesome and didn't mind, but I really felt terrible when I said yes and couldn't help plan or make the bachelorette party or the wedding shower. Shooting the show twelve to fourteen hours a day takes up almost all of my time. Guilt, guilt, guilt . . . but she was cool with it. Someone asks for help—and I know they have high expectations of me—and I just take the bait. But you have to realize you can't please all the people all the time. You're not letting someone down by being practical. You're letting them down by disappointing them when you ditch them. Consider:

- Is this promise realistic? Do I have the time to commit?

- Why am I making this promise? What is my motivation?

- Am I expecting something in return for this promise?

- What is the consequence if I break this promise?

- What is my limit? Am I too overworked right now to make another promise?

5 minutes to glee
BE GENEROUS

Donate your time, money, and/or effort to someone or something in need. It makes you feel needed and gives you a purpose in life. Not sure where to start? Find a cause that is near and dear to your heart. I have worked with Oceana (http://oceana.org) for over two years now. The oceans and wildlife are very important to me, and this organization is dedicated to keeping them safe and clean. Two years ago, instead of birthday gifts I asked everyone to donate to them instead. I also recently auctioned off some of my dresses from my closet that I've worn to events like the *Twilight* premiere. Part of those proceeds went to Oceana as well. I volunteer with my friend Jess at a local kitchen preparing food like sandwiches and salads for the homeless. An hour makes a huge difference in people's lives, and it'll surprise you how good you feel after.

A NICE WAY TO SAY NO

Your friend says: "Can I borrow your lip gloss? I left mine at home."
You're thinking: "Eww! I'm a total germaphobe and the last thing I want is her spit in my mouth!"

You say: "I'm so sorry. I think I'm coming down with something, so it's probably not a good idea."

Your sister asks: "Can you PLEASE bake your famous chocolate chip cookies for my kid's school bake sale?"
You're thinking: "I barely have time during the day to pee. Do you think I have time to bake cookies?"

You say: "I'd love to help, but unfortunately I'm overextended. Can I e-mail you my recipe?"

Your boss says: "I'd like you to take on another project. It's due tomorrow a.m."
You're thinking: "Holy crap! Is she out of her mind? I'm not a machine!"

You say: "I truly appreciate your faith in me. But I have so much already on my plate at work that deserves my one-hundred percent attention. Maybe someone else isn't as busy?"

Your friend asks: "Would you mind if I bring a date to your bday bash?"
You're thinking: "It's costing me $100 a head—she's got some balls!"

You say: "I'm sorry, but the guest list is set. I know you understand."

Your brother says: "Can I borrow a couple hundred bucks? I need a new set of golf clubs."
You're thinking: "And I need my head examined if I lend you a nickel. You haven't paid me back the money you borrowed from when you were ten yet!"

You say: "I'm terribly sorry! I just blew all my money on your Christmas and birthday presents for this year. I'm broke!"

PROMISES, PROMISES

Make ONE promise to yourself today—even a small one—and keep it. Build your commitments slowly and check them off as you accomplish each one.

I,_____, hereby promise:

I, Jenna, hereby promise

To be more open and honest with people

To try something that scares me.

To continue working out and taking good care of my body

To make sure that I devote at least an hour a day to do something I want to do for me.

To do my vocal warm ups at least four times a week

To go to the gym at least three times a week

To eat my vegetables once a day

To be more frugal with my money and not buy every pair of shoes that call to me!

171

> "To die would be an awfully big adventure!"
> —PETER PAN

RULE 9
JUMP IN!

i remember when Chris, Heather, and I got into our black leotards the day we were shooting "Single Ladies" the first season of *Glee*. I looked over at Chris in his fabulously sparkly vest, tie, and gloves. He had barely come out to his friends and family members, and now he was about to come out to 11 million people on national television!

I put my arm around him. I was a little worried. "You know things are going to be very different after this episode when Kurt comes out to his dad."

He smiled. "I know." Then he got up, did the number, and blew us all away.

And that, my friends, is what I call courage—to risk everything so that other kids can be comfortable with coming out; to show the LGBT community that it's okay to be who you are, loud and proud. Chris had been bullied before; he wasn't sure he wouldn't be bullied again. But it didn't matter to him. He had a bigger goal, a larger purpose in life. And it was worth taking this leap of faith to achieve it.

It didn't take long for him to become a role model for the young gay community—and to earn an Emmy nomination. His family and friends were as proud as I was. Any time I'm worried about entering uncharted territory, I think of Chris. He takes risks with guts and grace. All I have to do is hum a few bars of "Single Ladies" and I find my backbone!

If you don't take the risk, you won't learn. I've figured out that putting your ass on the line is truly the best way to grow and evolve. It helps you see what you're really made of! If I had to choose one huge whopper of a risk, it would be going on tour for *Glee*. I did some mini-tours with the Broadway Kids, but small-town auditoriums and malls can't compare to the Gibson Amphitheatre in LA. It was insane traveling on a bus or plane, waking up in a succession of strange hotel rooms, and

Chris is my role model for taking risks with guts and grace.

performing live in front of thousands of screaming fans. When you film a musical number on *Glee* and you screw it up, you can shoot it again . . . and again . . . and again, till it's it perfect. On tour, there is no "again." It's all in the moment—like lightning. If you trip and fall or forget the lyrics, there's no do-over. That is scary! Just to put it into perspective, 485,000 people saw our 2011 concerts. We did forty shows. I can't even name all the cities we were in because it's all a blur. But one does stand out among the pack. . .

On our first tour, it was our first night at Radio City Music Hall in New York City. I normally drink about two bottles of water during a show and a Red Bull. I always have to pee right before the encore when I sing "True Colors." But for some reason, this time I couldn't hold it. I was crossing my legs, trying my best not to pee in my pants. There was no way I was going to make it to the bathroom all the way up the stairs and down the hall in time for my big solo. So, my costumer Lizzie kicked everyone out of the changing room under the stage and handed me a bucket.

"Go for it," she said. "A lot of singers do it."

I stared at her. "Seriously? You want me to pee in there?"

Lizzie nodded. "They all do." I could see Mick Jagger or Springsteen taking a leak in a pail. But Taylor Swift? Barbra Streisand? Nuh-uh!

I hesitated, then seized the porta-pail from Lizzie's hands and did my business. There wasn't even a roll of Charmin in sight. But hey, I made it back seconds before the intro to the song started. Glam it wasn't, but it saved me from making a puddle onstage.

Even in my relationships, if I hadn't taken the leap and made a few mistakes along the way, I wouldn't be the strong woman I am today who now has an *amazing* boyfriend. I wouldn't know how to handle a relationship like I can

now. I believe that as hard as it is, heartbreak opens the heart. I remember my first breakup, I lost about 10 pounds, couldn't hold food down, couldn't sleep and didn't want to talk to anyone, so I went home to my parents' house and cocooned there for a while. While I was home, I realized how much love I had for my family. The breakup might have caused a hole in my heart, but it could be filled with love from my friends and family. Each breakup is different for me because each relationship has taught me something different.

"Joe" taught me the most. I learned how to stand up for myself and never let anyone make me feel little or less of a person just because I was too scared to stand up for myself.

When I was twenty-one, and living in New York bartending, David taught me always to trust my gut. I knew he wasn't looking for something serious, but I was, so I had to get out because I knew I'd get hurt. I had to think of me. I later found out he was seeing quite a few people at the same time and was never going to commit to any one of us. Don't I feel smart for following my instincts!

Next came "Larry." At this point, I was twenty-three and coming into my own. From him I learned the importance of never settling. If you feel like you're at 50 percent with someone and that's as far as you'll get, you're wasting precious time. You should always be with someone who enriches your life and inspires you to be the best you can be.

SPLITSVILLE

Love (or what you think is love) has this bad habit of putting blinders on you. I dated a guy once—let's call him Joe. Throughout our year and a half together, I compromised who I was way too many times. I never spoke my opinion; I always indulged him to the point where I no longer had a thought in my head that wasn't his. I lost friends because he couldn't deal with sharing me. I felt myself—the person I knew I was inside—dying to come out, but I was too scared to do it. He was pulling me away from all the people I loved and cared about. He manipulated me into believing my best friend at the time betrayed him and made me choose between them. He spoke badly about my family and the way I was brought up. He would criticize how my family spent their money; he would nitpick their lifestyle. He would compare me to his past relationship. (I never could measure up.) He'd tell me things I did or said were stupid. Well, I'll admit to being stupid over one thing—staying in this bad romance. I should have seen it coming. I felt lost and attacked in this relationship all the time. Where had I gone?

Finally, I realized I was better than this, and I deserved better than him (and I told him so). It took a culmination of a lot of things to bring me to this point. Basically, I was a ticking time bomb ready to explode. He called me "stupid" one day and that was the last straw. It wasn't just that I couldn't have an opinion but also that he clearly had a negative opinion about me. So I told him I couldn't do it anymore. Nobody calls me stupid. I walked out, never looking back. And I could finally breathe.

I'm not proud of this relationship or of how I behaved at this time in my life. I'm not proud that I didn't speak up and tell him that he was wrong. But it made me a stronger person, and I learned the kind of person he is. (Note to self: Avoid this type in the future!) It took being silenced to find my voice. Nobody will ever take it from me again.

WHAT MAKES A GOOD RELATIONSHIP

- He/she is a best friend.
- He/she challenges you every day and makes you smile all the time.
- It's a two-way street; both partners work at it and communicate.
- You better each other while never losing what's inside *you*.
- You see the world in a new way.

I met my best friend/my other half, my boyfriend, Michael Trevino at Comic Con in San Diego a few years ago. I was there for *Glee*, and he was there for *Vampire Diaries* (in case you didn't know, he plays "hybrid" Tyler Lockwood). I wasn't even looking for a boyfriend. He came along, and our conversation was effortless, and he made me laugh. It just clicked. When you know something feels right, it's like another puzzle piece to your life fits in. I love that he reminds me every day not to take myself too seriously. He's showed me that no matter what, it's crucial to stay in the moment and really take in what is around you. He teaches me loyalty and gratitude and opens my heart to him and to new things every day. I am a more open and honest person because of him, and he keeps me grounded. I think that we bounce off each other and our energy. We remind each other to live life to the fullest and most importantly to have fun.

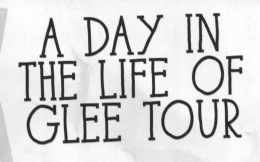

A DAY IN THE LIFE OF GLEE TOUR

Wake up in Chicago

Call Kevin

Go eat breakfast

Go sightseeing or, in our case, shopping

Back to hotel

Shower

Pack your bag and leave it by your door
to be picked up

Meet in the lobby

Go to the van that is taking us
to the arena

Get a rundown of where
everything is in the arena

Eat lunch/dinner

Soundcheck

Get hair and makeup done

Stretch, get dressed

Hang out in common room

SHOW CIRCLE

Walk to stage

Pick up your mic

SHOWTIME

Curtain

Change

Eat a snack at the arena
(deep-dish pizza in Chicago)

Get on the bus . . .
(dance party on the bus!)

Get to airport

Get on flight

Land in next city

Check into hotel

Maybe go for a swim if there's a
hotel pool or see if there's a hotel
bar

Sleep

Wake up....

Do it all over again!

I asked some of my castmates to describe tour in three words. Here are some of their responses:

CHORD: nerves, excitement, experience

HEATHER: booze, dancing, friends

DARREN: once in a lifetime (That's four!)

KEVIN: exhausting, thrilling, perfect

CORY: exhilarating, intense, life-changing

when you leap . . .
you sometimes fall

Failure hurts. I won't kid you . . . rejection is a bitch. And it's hard not to take that kind of stuff personally. If some casting agent insinuated (or told me outright) that I wasn't pretty or skinny enough, or my acting didn't read well, it hurt like hell. I got really close for the part of Christmas Eve in *Avenue Q* while I was in college . . . and also for the role of Nelly Yuki on *Gossip Girl* while I was performing in *Spring Awakening* in 2008. I wanted both badly. I wanted *Gossip Girl* badly because I loved the show so much, and I had watched since the beginning. I was dying to do Broadway again and *Avenue Q* was so funny! But I was too young for Christmas Eve, and the role of Nelly on *Gossip Girl* ended up disappearing for a few seasons anyway. C'est la vie. No use crying over spilled milk or lost roles. No matter what trials and tribulations you face, you gotta keep on truckin'. In retrospect, the role on *Gossip Girl* would've overlapped with the time of *Glee* auditions, so I wouldn't have been able to do it!! See?!

> **Moving to LA to shoot *Glee* was a huge leap for me. I was basically leaving my entire life and family back on the other side of the country.**

shake things up

Change is good—scary yes, but good. Moving to LA to shoot *Glee* was a huge leap for me. I was basically leaving my entire life and family back on the other side of the country. I'd never been more than 30 miles from the home where I grew up. I rented an apartment without seeing it—big mistake. It was dark, cold, and on the tenth floor. The elevator was dark and creaky and barely worked. The lights flickered, and the pipes were rusted. The paint and plaster were peeling off the walls. I looked around: It now sort of reminds me of something out of *American Horror Story*. I sat on the cold toilet bowl and cried. I think I was in shock over everything that was happening and changing so quickly. Eventually, I calmed down. I needed to just let things settle down. I wanted instant gratification, and that wasn't going to happen. My parents came out and helped me set up my apartment, and I made so many friends on *Glee*. So it all just clicked. I just needed to give it some time.

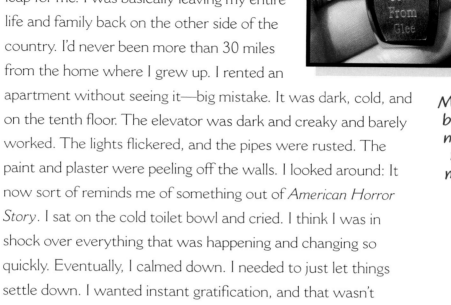

My parents bought this necklace for me when I moved to LA.

"There is a Greek expression, 'If you're going to join the dance circle, then you must dance.' Many of us walk around the circle but never join in. You can't be happy on the outside of anything. The longer you sit out of life, the harder it is to get in. Sometimes you just have to close your eyes and dance Zorba's dance with your fat aunt."

—John Stamos 183

try it . . . you might like it

It's like when I was a kid and my mom said, "Eat your broccoli trees," I would stick up my nose and push the plate away. But eventually, I realized they're not too bad. Same goes for life; give anything a shot *just once* if you think the payoff is worth it. Everything is a risk:

To live is to risk dying
To love is to risk being rejected
To try is to risk failing
To hope is to risk being disappointed

But I truly believe that the person who risks nothing does nothing, has nothing, and *is* nothing. Being young is about testing your boundaries. You are becoming an independent adult, and you don't simply want to explore your limits—you want to bust out of them. You want to nurture your spirit, push your body, and expand your mind! But all risks are not equal. . . .

184

SMART RISKS TO TAKE

- a new sport
- a new hobby
- an elective in school you're curious about
- learning a new language
- joining a new club
- doing something selfless for someone else
- buying a place
- going to a party where you don't know anyone
- having your first dinner party when you're new to cooking!

STUPID RISKS TO TAKE

- drinking under age
- DUI
- drugs
- running with the wrong crowd
- running away from your problems
- running with scissors
- starving yourself to lose weight
- unprotected sex

SHOPLIFTING

When I was in high school, I shoplifted. I stole a wallet for myself and one for my friend, and it was the dumbest thing I could've done. I risked my student council presidency at school and my record. It was in our local mall, and when I walked out of the store, the buzzer went off. The girl checked my bag and found the wallets hidden in one of my shopping bags. The cops came and had to take me to the station. Yes, I've ridden in a cop car. I never thought I'd get caught, and maybe I wanted to show off to my friend. The crazy thing is, we actually had the money to buy the wallets. I had heard that all my other friends shoplifted at least once in their life, and I wanted to join the club.

Luckily, I was still considered a minor so all the charges went away, but I paid. I was punished by my parents severely: No friends, TV, telephone, or anything for a week. I was so embarrassed as people walked by in the store and saw me sitting in the corner with mall security. My own guilt was enough to teach me a powerful lesson.

185

5 minutes to glee

Get CRAFTY

Remember when you were a kid and you loved to finger paint? Messy, yes, but also liberating! Expressing yourself artistically is a wonderful way to brighten your day. I know a lot of actors who knit. It makes them happy, and I've received quite a few lovely scarves as a result! Get yourself into one of those paint-a-pot places and channel your inner Picasso. (Doesn't everyone need a colorful cereal bowl or a mug?) Or make a scrapbook of your fave photos and decorate the pages with silly jots and doodles. I also think it's fun to snap artsy photos on Instagram or Twitter and share them. Personally, some of my fave pics have been of my nails, my shoes, and my lunch. Annie Leibovitz, eat your heart out!

187

RULE 10
TAKE A BOW

"LET'S SET THE WORLD ON FIRE, WE CAN BURN BRIGHTER THAN THE SUN."

—FUN., "WE ARE YOUNG"

applause, applause . . . we all need to hear it in one way or another. If you've come this far, it's time to give yourself a pat on the back. Even if you're not 100 percent at your destination, you've moved forward. It's about the journey, not the end point. I call my mom and dad when something great happens. I'll grab a glass of champagne, or go to a really nice dinner, or reward myself with something I've wanted to purchase. Give yourself credit where it's due. It's not egotistical to acknowledge your achievements. Sometimes you can overlook them when you leap from one challenge into the next. You've earned it. You've persevered. You've powered through. If I don't celebrate myself, then my friends certainly do. They constantly remind me of why I am where I am; they lift me up and push me to climb. They knew it, even if I didn't.

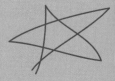

savor the simple joys

It isn't all about the big win. Sometimes, the little things are worth celebrating as well. Appreciate the peace, beauty, and stillness in your life on a daily basis. Stop and smell the roses. Little things make me happy, like Diet Coke with a straw, a text from someone I haven't heard from in a while, cuddling under the covers all day with Michael when it's raining outside, *Titanic* on TV, a tweet reply from someone I am a fan of, a new comfy blanket, or finding five dollars in my jeans pocket. They're such simple things, and you don't think about them because you just do them. But you need to, once in a while, just appreciate what makes you happy.

Dear Tina,
This is your time to come out of the shadows and shine! Do not be afraid to go find yourself. Take a journey and find the glee within. Search for the things that will make you feel the happiest and most complete. I have seen you evolve so much in the last four years from a quiet stuttering Goth to a bright young woman, unafraid to open herself up to joy, friends, and new experiences. This is no time to be scared! Take a risk: ask someone out, assert your opinions, enjoy shopping for a new dress. You're in your senior year so enjoy the lasts of everything. The last time you'll walk through the halls of McKinley. Bask in the joy of those moments. I know the break-up with Mike hurt like hell, but it made you realize the chances you've missed. I want you to see that good can come from bad. Appreciate what you DO have that makes you smile and laugh instead of worrying about the things you don't. I know you can do it... The sky's the limit. Break a leg and make me proud!

Love,
Jenna

rock the future!

Embrace it! Get excited about what it will hold. Don't rest on your laurels or ever stop challenging yourself to keep dreaming and moving forward. It's fun for two hours to have our fans make us feel like rock stars at *Glee Live!* onstage. The rush and the energy are like nothing else. But after our final bow, I'm backstage and back to being just Jenna. I also think the intense, demanding job of putting on a weekly musical TV show helps keep us all pretty grounded: There's no glamour in it. We work hard! When its 1:00 a.m. and you're trying to keep your eyes open and remember your lines after working for thirteen hours, it's not glamorous. When you're shooting a food fight in the cafeteria and they have to dump buckets of spaghetti and meatballs and Jell-O on your head, it's not glamorous. And finally, when you get slapped with an icy-cold slushie that goes up your nose and down your bra, it's not glamorous! But I wouldn't give it up for anything in the world.

good vibrations

Everyone radiates energy—good or bad—and it impacts greatly how our lives go. I'm a big believer in whatever you put out there, you get back in return (and then some.) That's the old law of attraction in action. When you project positive energy, you attract positive results in everything from work and relationships to your health. When you project your inner light outward, it has an amazing ripple effect. I know this has a New Agey, Star Treky ring to it—like I'm asking you to shoot off a beam of light. But what I'm talking about is more of an attitude adjustment. Embody the positivity you wish to see in the world. Let your heart be light and your eyes have a twinkle. If you think all of this is spiritual mumbo jumbo, try hanging out with someone who has a chip on his shoulder. In minutes, you'll probably feel as cranky and crabby as he does—or you'll wanna flee for cover. That's his energy encompassing your space. The same goes for being around someone who lets his/her inner light shine through. Jonathan Groff is one of those people. We met

> "Happiness is working hard at what you love."
> —JONATHAN GROFF

194

when we were both on Broadway doing *Spring Awakening*. He shook my hand and his face lit up in a smile. I instantly felt warm and welcome in his presence, as if we'd known each other our whole lives. He's a happy and hardworking guy, and he puts forth that happiness in an incredibly generous way.

Here's how to project your own positivity:

Be a problem-solver. If a difficult situation comes up, keep your cool and say, "No problema. We can fix this!" Be the one who tries to solve the problem—not the one who dwells on it.

Don't bitch. Brooding isn't attractive on anyone—unless you're Stefan on *Vampire Diaries*. Chronic complainers are not fun to be around. When someone starts to whine, that's usually my cue to leave.

Say yes. These three little letters have so much positivity! You don't have to do it always, but at least answer in the affirmative once in a while. It shows people you're willing to pitch in and can be counted on.

Let someone else do the talking. Ask questions and make someone feel important; don't just monopolize the conversation. Since I'm a big talker, this is tough for me to do. I have to literally zip my lip and not interrupt. I have to remember that conversation is a dialogue, not a monologue!

"I'M JUST THE SAME AS I WAS . . ."
—IMAGINE DRAGONS, "IT'S TIME"

195

Express your joy: sing it, dance it, write about it, scream it from the rooftops. Allow it to fill you up and overflow! I love to dance and let the moment take me where I want to go. When I got the approval to go do the Gaga video, I think I danced and screamed and cheered around our living room in my pajamas. Kevin was a witness.

Cherish the people who are there for you in your life; never neglect your home team. Remember to look at the things and people that you *do* have in your life rather than harping on the things you don't. I look at every day as if everything could be taken away from me tomorrow. I really appreciate the gems in my life, the people who have rooted for me since the beginning through thick and thin. The ones who inspired me, pushed me, made me laugh, cry, smile, or sing. My home team are my parents Judi and Brad; my brother Gregg; my sister-in-law Kira; Michael; Mr. H; my manager Eric; my agents; and my best friends Dante, Matty, Jess, Kevin, and Cristy. They give me light, love, positivity, hope, and most of all, glee.

"Laughter is key. Dancing a must. Because oh, how we do love both things! But most important, posses the ability to be present, be true to your deepest wishes, intentions. Do good unto others, to yourself. Being true to yourself is one of the greatest attributes. Happiness ensues. Be present. Be kind. Be patient. Be honest. Find moments to be silly. The results will always be rewarding."

—DIANNA AGRON

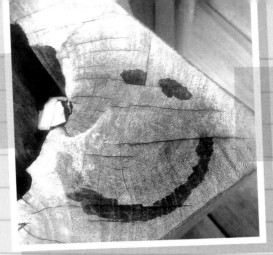

Look, my cup left a smiley face!

The glee inside of Me

Now that you know how to achieve your own personal brand of happiness, how will you carry it through your life?

Laugh every day. **Kids crack up about 500 times in 24 hours. (This is not something I am making up—it's a fact!) Adults only laugh 15 to 100 times. Make it your goal to giggle. It's good for mind, body, and soul.**

Surround yourself with happy people. **It's contagious. Look for individuals who are positive influences—who life you up and inspire you.**

Play hard; don't just work hard. **Allow yourself plenty of downtime to relax, get physical, get crazy.**

Write down your happy thoughts. **Keep a diary of joyful moments so they don't slip through your fingertips. Look back on them whenever you need a boost. This book will definitely do it for me!**

Celebrate the love in your life. **Love who you are, what you do, who you do it with, and where you're going.**

Compliment yourself for a job well done, a love well earned, a life well spent. **I'll start you out: "You rock!"**

NO SMOKING

BLUE BIRD

FELONY CHARGES MAY
BE FILED AGAINST ANY
PERSON(S)
COMMITTING AN
AGGRAVATED ASSAULT
OR
BATTERY UPON ANY
SCHOOL EMPLOYEE.

5 minutes to glee
GUILTY PLEASURES

Money cannot buy you happiness, but sometimes an expensive pair of shoes can put a smile on my face. (They don't call it retail therapy for nothing!) It's okay to indulge for a few minutes every day. Help yourself to seconds. Deep-condition your hair. Flip through a rag magazine and giggle over gossip. Me? I eat pizza in bed while I watch the Yankees or Giants recap on the evening news. You get the point? Do what makes you feel good—and a little guilty—every now and then. Treat yourself—you deserve it!

Hi, my name is Jenna, and I'm a shoe-a-holic.

199

i am a person who doesn't just talk the talk; I walk the walk. Meaning I have lived with my own personal "glee project" for over two years now, mulling over every bit of advice I've laid out for you in the previous chapters. I truly believe in each and every one of these principles. I put them into action every day of my life, striving to find peace and joy in everything I do and in every way I do it. When I first suggested writing a book about choosing glee in your life, I was met with lots of furrowed brows. Surely you can't choose your own happiness! You can't control your own destiny! You can't create your own success!

Yes you can . . . and yes, you should. I'm living proof. It's as simple as defining what you want and steering a course for it. The more I asked people what makes them happy, the more I began to build my own happiness list. (Thanks everyone, for the great advice!) These are the things that make me giggle, that take me to a lighter, brighter place. I try to add a few more to the list every day. Here's what I have so far:

- Watching television all day long

- A burrito that doesn't fall apart while you're eating it

- A new pair of heels almost too high to walk in

- Disney movie marathons

- Sitting around the dinner table with my mom, dad, and brother like old times

- Date nights with Michael

- Puppies that roll on their back and can't get up

- A really good challenging day at work with a great scene partner

- Going to a karaoke bar with the *Glee* cast and singing myself silly

- Seeing someone with my book in their hands (SMILE)

"Happiness is something you live... a collective combination of big, small, concrete, abstract things in life that are defined uniquely for every person's path."

~Darren Criss

Make Your Own Happiness List

Carry it with you on your iPhone, keep it tacked to your fridge, or tuck it in your purse on a slip of paper. Just keep on adding to it every single day. And then, whenever you need it, reread what you've written and let it lift you up. The point is to record your happiness wherever you go, whenever you find it. This is about being in the moment and recognizing that every moment is an opportunity to choose glee.

My Top 10 Favorite Glee Moments (in no particular order)

1. Singing my first solo on the show, "True Colors"

2. Vampire Tina

3. Stepping out onto the Radio City stage for the first time, and selling out five shows there (OMG!)

4. Singing for the First Lady and President Obama on The White House lawn

5. Watching Amber sing the National Anthem on The White House lawn

6. Sharing my first on-screen kiss with Kevin McHale

7. Oprah ('nuf said)

8. Doing "Don't Stop Believin'" seventy-five times and counting to get it right during the pilot

9. Wathing the show on Fox for the very first time at Lea Michele's house and seeing "Don't Stop" go to #1 on the charts immediately after

10. Shooting a Superbowl commercial, going to the Superbowl and working on a Superbowl episode!

I owe you a big thank you for reading this book—you are a big part of my happiness because you gave me a reason to write it. Because of you, I sat down, reexamined my life, and connected the dots. I took great notes, doodled, dictated, and in the end, handed in a whopping 40,000 words. Honestly, for a girl who struggled to write a 1,000-word essay in college, that is impressive! I really had a lot to say, and I'm proud of myself. I'm also proud of the journey. In case you've ever wondered, writing a book is like several months of therapy. You just keep talking till it makes sense and the pieces fall into place.

Now—because I'm never just satisfied with sitting back and relaxing—I'm already thinking, "What's next?"—I'd love to turn my choosing glee project into a lifelong mission. I'd like to continue spreading the word and inspiring people to chart a course to their own happiness. I'd love to explore ideas, dreams, and talents—I know I have them in here somewhere. Yours may be very different from mine—and that's the beauty of it. You can't bottle happiness; you can't prescribe it. All you can do is follow your heart and soul where it takes you. Now we both know what to do and how to do it. So what are you waiting for? An invitation? Well, here it is:

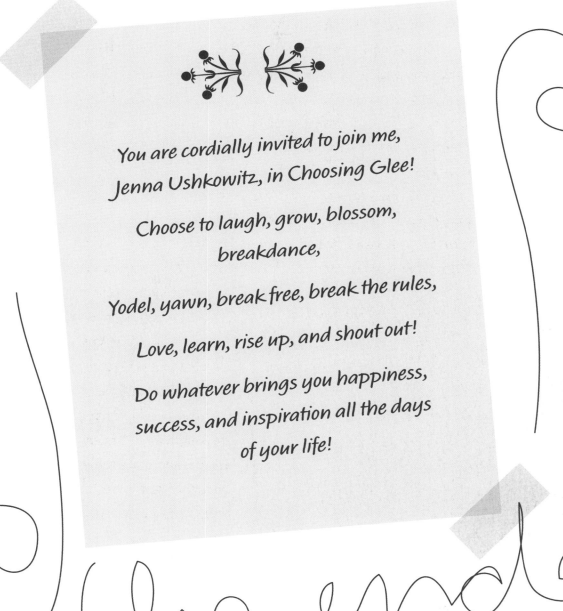

You are cordially invited to join me, Jenna Ushkowitz, in Choosing Glee!

Choose to laugh, grow, blossom, breakdance,

Yodel, yawn, break free, break the rules,

Love, learn, rise up, and shout out!

Do whatever brings you happiness, success, and inspiration all the days of your life!

the end

209

JENNA
9

213

215

ACKNOWLEDGMENTS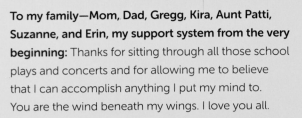

To my family—Mom, Dad, Gregg, Kira, Aunt Patti, Suzanne, and Erin, my support system from the very beginning: Thanks for sitting through all those school plays and concerts and for allowing me to believe that I can accomplish anything I put my mind to. You are the wind beneath my wings. I love you all.

To my amazing team—Eric Emery, Ellen Gilbert, Rachel Altman, Bonnie Schumofsky, Steve Ross: For always pushing for me and for believing in me enough to write *Choosing Glee*. And Eric . . . here's to always getting things done.

To my writing partner, Sheryl Berk: This book would not be what it is without you. Thank you for helping me find my voice and for your patience, enthusiasm, and encouragement.

To my very patient editor, Kathryn Huck and the team at St. Martin's Press—Kate Ottaviano, Loren Jaggers, Matthew Shear, and Joseph Goldshein: I am eternally grateful to you for taking a chance on me and *Choosing Glee*. I couldn't have asked for a better publisher and editor. Thank you for bringing my passion project to life.

To Stonesong: Your diligence and hustle does not go unnoticed. I appreciate every second you spent making this book so beautiful and for far exceeding my every expectation.

To the best glam team and photographer— Jeff Katz, Theodore Leaf, Patrick DeFontbrune, Amanda Reno, Shannon McClure, Mazik Saevitz: For making my cover shoot a success. Thank you for always making me feel comfortable and beautiful. You're the dream team!

To my Guardian Angels—PMK, Michael Gagliardo, Brit Reece, Kelley Kirkpatrick, and Jill Fritzo: Thanks for always protecting me, taking care of me, and always making me laugh.

To Ryan Murphy, Brad Falchuk, Ian Brennan, Dante Di Loreto, and my amazing, wonderful, talented, *Glee* family: Thank you for taking me on the journey of a lifetime. I would not be who I am today without each and every one of you.

To my rock, Michael Trevino: my heart, my best friend and confidante. Thank you for loving me for me. . . . I love you.

To my partner in crime, Dante Russo: Thank you for your patience, advice and friendship. Here's to the endless texts, e-mails, and phone calls and to dealing with my crazy during this process. . . . I couldn't have done it without you.

To the Best Friends in the entire world (even the ones 3,000 miles away): Matty, Cristy, Blake, Jess, Will, Emma, Kev, Tara, Chris, Kellie, Kelly, Adrien, Alexis MW, Donna M, and Manny and Helen.

To my own personal Mr. Schuester, Jim Hoare, "JH," My Mentor and Protector: Thank you for teaching me to never cut corners and to take risks. You helped me gain the confidence to achieve my dreams. "Think. Believe. Dream. Dare"

Thank you to everyone close to my heart who contributed their hearts to this book. It wouldn't be the same without you: Kevin McHale, Vanessa Lengies, Darren Criss, Chris Colfer, Dianna Agron, Harry Shum, Lea Michele, Amber Riley, Becca Tobin, Cory Monteith, Chord Overstreet, Heather Morris, Naya Rivera, Brad Falchuk, Zach Woodlee, Adam Shankman, Ryan Murphy, John Stamos, Kristin Chenoweth, Jessica Szhor, Michael Trevino, Nina Dobrev, Matthew Maisto, Dante Russo, Jon Groff, Blake Bashoff, Adrien Finkle, Brad Ushkowitz, Judi Ushkowitz, Gregg Lariosa, Jim Hoare.

And thank you Adam Rose, for all the beautiful *Glee* photos.